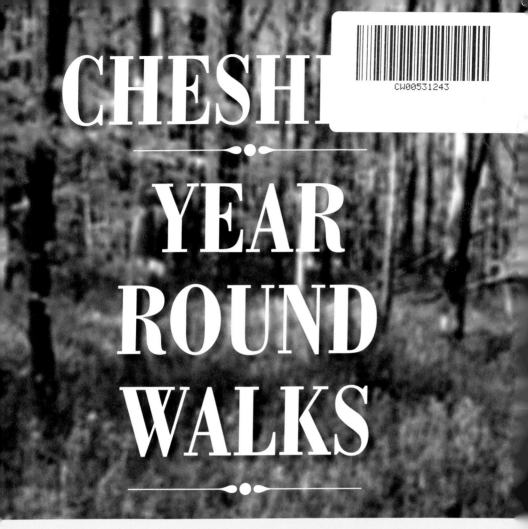

CHESHI
YEAR
ROUND
WALKS

Spring, Summer, Autumn & Winter

Judy Smith

COUNTRYSIDE BOOKS
NEWBURY BERKSHIRE

COUNTRYSIDE BOOKS
3 Catherine Road
Newbury
Berkshire

To view our complete range of books please visit us at
www.countrysidebooks.co.uk

ISBN 978 1 84674 360 3

All materials used in the production of this book carry FSC certification.

Photographs by Judy Smith

Produced by The Letterworks Ltd., Reading
Typeset by KT Designs, St Helens
Printed by The Holywell Press, Oxford

Contents

Contents

Autumn

Winter

Introduction

In times past, we lived closer to the earth and to the seasons than we do today. In the long nights of winter, people went to bed early; with daylight and warmth increasing, they planted crops to be harvested in summer and autumn; what could be stored was saved for use over winter. There were no televisions providing entertainment for the dark hours, no supermarkets offering peaches in January and Brussels sprouts in July, no jets to whisk us off for a quick dose of winter sunshine, no cruise liners carrying us to Arctic glaciers at the height of summer. The cycle of the year was all-important, and traditional celebrations like Midsummer, Michaelmas and Yuletide brought a sense of rhythm and continuity. We can't do much about the complexity of our lives today, but maybe we would do well to relate more to the year's natural changes. This book pays homage to just that idea.

Here are twenty routes intended to showcase the best of each season. In spring, you can enjoy bluebells, apple blossom and herons' nests; in summer, the seaside, and the heights of Cheshire's Peak District. Autumn brings deep-bronzed beech woods and forest feasts, while at the end of the year there are winter visitors on the estuary, and woods filling up with snow. The walks are not long – they range between two and eight miles in length – because, for the most part, they are what I call 'stand and stare' walks.

On short walks like these, you should have time to 'stand and stare' – to stare at Cheshire spread before you from Shutlingsloe's summit, to admire the carpet of snowdrops at Dunham Massey, to scan the waters off Hilbre Island for seals, to hunt for fungi in the woods – and to sit down with a Snugburys ice cream!

If you are feeling bold, you could set yourself the challenge of taking every walk in this book in the coming year. Cheshire is a lovely county, and should you happen to get addicted as you explore, it's no matter, because with every walk there are suggestions for other routes that are similar. And most significantly, with every walk there are ideas for refreshment as well. That 'cup of tea and piece of cake' is surely an important part of the walking experience!

I do hope you enjoy the round of the year in Cheshire. I wish you good luck on your travels.

Judy Smith

DEDICATION

For our grandson, Xander. One day, may you also get to wander through the seasons in lovely Cheshire.

My thanks go to Eric for all his patience and support. 'They also serve who only stand and wait' is very true!

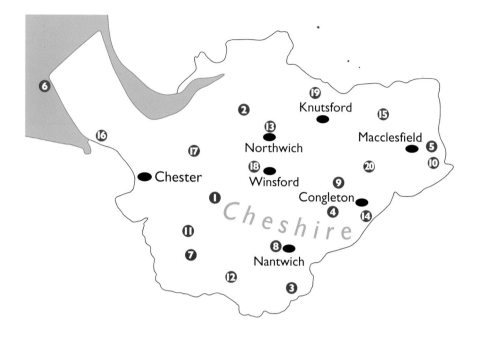

PUBLISHER'S NOTE

We hope that you obtain considerable enjoyment from this book; great care has been taken in its preparation. In order to assist in navigation to the start point of the walk, we have included the nearest postcode, although of course a postcode cannot always deliver you to a precise starting point, especially in rural areas. Although at the time of publication all routes followed public rights of way or permitted paths, diversion orders can be made and permissions withdrawn.

We cannot, of course, be held responsible for such diversion orders or any inaccuracies in the text which result from these or any other changes to the routes, nor any damage which might result from walkers trespassing on private property. We are anxious, though, that all the details covering the walks are kept up to date, and would therefore welcome information from readers which would be relevant to future editions.

The simple sketch maps that accompany the walks in this book are based on notes made by the author whilst surveying the routes on the ground. They are designed to show you how to reach the start and to point out the main features of the overall circuit, and they contain a progression of numbers that relate to the paragraphs of the text.

However, for the benefit of a proper map, we do recommend that you purchase the relevant Ordnance Survey sheet covering your walk. Ordnance Survey maps are widely available, especially through booksellers and local newsagents.

Looking out over Lancashire from Old Pale

1 *Kelsall*

7 miles (11.2 km)

This walk sets out from the woodland car park entitled Gresty's Waste. Some people say that this land, or 'waste', once belonged to a man called Gresty, while others declare it was definitely a one-time badger run (from the Old English *graegstig*). Whatever your view, this oddly named place sits cosily between attractive Delamere Forest, in the north of the county, and the fruit and cattle-farming heartlands in the south. The route here takes in both scenarios, and is surely at its best in springtime, when the apple trees are in blossom, the woodland floor is carpeted with bluebells and stitchwort, and the fertile soil ensures an exuberance of colour in every wayside garden.

Having said that, there's so much more of interest on this walk that it is well worth taking at any time of year. In the woods you can seek out a 'hanging stone' where deer thieves once met their end; later on, there is the bizarre rock formation of Urchin's Kitchen. On the path down pretty Boothsdale, there are distant prospects of the Shropshire Hills, the Breiddens and the Welsh mountains, while the view of seven counties from the summit of Old Pale Hill is one not to be missed.

Terrain Forest paths and tracks, and some minor roads.

Map OS Explorer 267 Northwich & Delamere Forest.

Starting point Gresty's Waste free car park (GR SJ 540686).

How to get there & parking Gresty's Waste car park is signed on the A54, about eight miles east of Chester, near the village of Kelsall. **Sat Nav:** CW6 0SP.

Refreshments The walk passes two pubs, the Farmers Arms at Kelsall ☎ 01829 751480 www.farmersarmskelsall.co.uk, and the Boot Inn at Willington ☎ 01829 751375 www.thebootinnwillington.com.

The Walk

1 From the top corner of **Gresty's Waste** car park, cross the A54 with the greatest care. Walk up the broad forest track opposite (signed '**Sandstone Trail**'), and in about 150 metres, take the first path on the right (signed '**Stoney Lane**'). Very shortly, just before the stile leaving the forest, take a track on the left that soon leads into an old hillside quarry. The hill here is known as **Hangingstone Hill**: Delamere was once a royal hunting forest, and it is said that one of these rocks was used to hang those unwise enough to steal the king's deer. No one seems to know which rock, though! The quarry itself was given the name 'King's Chair'. Walk right through the quarry, and descend to the main track again. Turn right here, and continue a short distance to a cross-tracks where a wooden post bears the number 2.

2 Turn right here, and keep to the main track, which soon bends left to climb uphill. Keep ahead to another junction (Post 3). Ahead of you now is the summit viewpoint, with a stone showing the direction of each county. Walk round the viewpoint to Post 8, and leave on the track between the stones for Derbyshire and Staffordshire. In 250 metres, at Post 7, turn right and continue to meet a tarmacked lane (Post 4).

3 Turn right, and in about fifty metres, take a wide, grassy track on the left. Keep ahead on this (ignore a field-side track on the left), walking downhill to a five-way junction. Turn right here, and very soon you will reach the track you were on earlier; keep ahead to return to Post 2. Now take the track straight ahead, which soon leaves the wood and becomes a tarmacked lane. Go straight over the first crossroads, and continue to the second (with a car park opposite).

spring

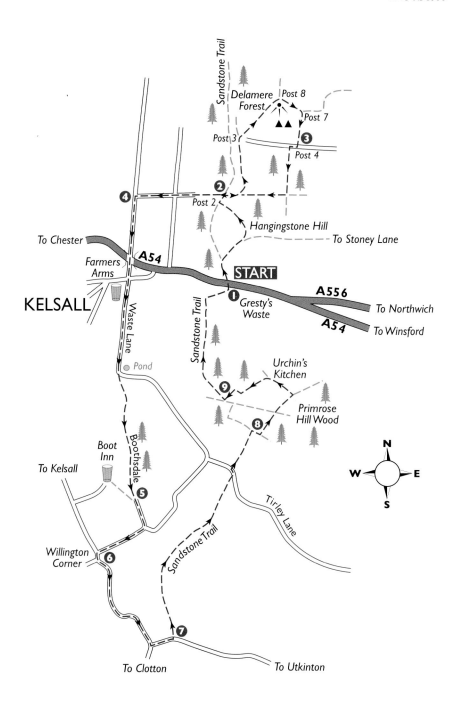

Sandstone Trail

Delamere Forest · Post 8

Post 7

Post 3

❸

Post 4

❹ ← **❷**

Post 2

Hangingstone Hill

To Stoney Lane

To Chester

Farmers Arms

A54

START

KELSALL

❶ Gresty's Waste

A556

To Northwich

A54

To Winsford

Waste Lane

Sandstone Trail

Pond

Urchin's Kitchen

❾

Primrose Hill Wood

❽

Boothsdale

Boot Inn

To Kelsall

❺

N

W   E

S

Willington Corner

❻

Tirley Lane

Sandstone Trail

❼

To Clotton

To Utkinton

The Boot Inn at Willington.

4 Turn left on a road passing over the A54 to a crossroads beside the **Farmers Arms**. Go straight over into **Waste Lane**, and walk gradually uphill. After almost ½ mile, the road swings left at a corner with a pond and a seat. Take the track ahead here, keeping to the right after the white house on a path signposted to **Willington**. Through a kissing gate, the track runs alongside fields, then dips abruptly down steps into **Boothsdale**. Continue on this narrow path, enjoying the views. The abrupt bump ahead is **Breidden Hill** with the craggy Shropshire Hills to the left and the Welsh hills to the right.

5 Where the path meets a lane beside a modern house, a path on the right leads to the inviting **Boot Inn**. If you don't wish to stop here, continue to a T-junction and turn right. On the corner, at one time, was Willington Fruit Farm, which was in the care of the Wilson family for more than half a century. Sadly, today's economic climate has taken its toll on this area's fruit farms. Continue to the junction beside the green at **Willington Corner**.

6 Turn left here, and walk along the road for half a mile, taking great care – it can be busy. At the first junction, turn left (signposted to **Utkinton**) and continue for 200 metres to a fingerpost indicating the **Sandstone Trail**.

7 Turn left here, and follow this narrowing sandy lane uphill for almost a mile to arrive at a road (**Tirley Lane**). Turn left, and in fifty metres, at the corner, keep ahead on the path alongside the house. Continue, following the **Sandstone Trail** alongside fields and then down into **Primrose Hill Wood** through a kissing gate.

8 Turn right here (leaving the Sandstone Trail), and in fifty metres, take a path on the left. Reaching a forest road, cross straight over to take the broad, descending road opposite. Continue to where this leaves the wood on the left-hand side, and here take a track leading back to the left. After weaving its way along the woodland edge, this suddenly dips down to cross a stream on logs. Immediately afterwards, take a path left above the stream; it will lead you through the rocky, fern-hung gully known as **Urchin's Kitchen**. This deep cleft in the rock is, in origin, a glacial drainage channel. Forests were considered to be places of magic, and the word urchin here refers to the forest elves. Immediately after this, bear right to climb out of the gully, and on reaching a track crossroads, turn left. Continue to reach a wide forest track.

9 Here, turn sharp right on a narrow path, again joining the signed **Sandstone Trail**, which you will now follow back to **Gresty's Waste**. At the top of the hill, turn right, soon leaving the wood to walk alongside the end of the racecourse, and then dropping down through the trees to cross a stream on a wooden bridge. Wooden steps now take you back up to the car park.

What to look out for –

Old Pale Hill

At 176 metres, Old Pale Hill is the highest point of the northern part of Cheshire's long sandstone ridge, and it makes a splendid viewpoint. The main features of the landscape are indicated around the circumference of the raised area.

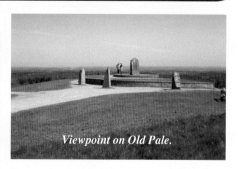
Viewpoint on Old Pale.

If you have enjoyed this walk

You might be keen to walk more of the Sandstone Trail. It's just thirty-four miles long and easily divided into sections. Download a comprehensive guide to the trail from www.sandstoneridge.org.uk/doc/D225692.pdf , or seek out a copy in local bookshops.

The bluebell wood at Bluebell Cottage Gardens and Nursery.

2 *Dutton*

4 or 2½ miles (6.4 or 4 km)

To see a wood thickly carpeted with bluebells is surely a glimpse of heaven. Unfortunately, those lovely flowers have a very short season of about three weeks. To ensure you don't miss it, take this ramble sometime around the beginning of May, and you will be in for a real treat.

The walk starts at Bluebell Cottage, a nursery and garden as charming as the name implies, and with its own bluebell wood alongside. The route goes on to skirt the River Weaver, and then returns along the Trent and Mersey Canal; in all that time there's scarcely a moment when there's not some blue somewhere in sight. But of course, bluebells are not the only flowers around: there are wood anemones, celandines, red campion, lady's smock and many other spring flowers to enjoy in this gentle, peaceful corner of Cheshire.

Terrain Woodland paths, hard-surfaced riverside track, canal towpath.

Map OS Explorer 267 Northwich & Delamere Forest.

Starting point Bluebell Cottage Gardens and Nursery (GR SJ 582779). Outside Bluebell Cottage's opening times you could start the walk instead at the Leigh Arms on the A49 Warrington–Whitchurch road, immediately north of the Acton Swing Bridge at Bartington (Point 4 in the walk) (GR SJ 601761).

How to get there & parking Situated on Lodge Lane, Bluebell Cottage Gardens and Nursery is clearly signed off the A533 Northwich–Runcorn road about a mile south of the village of Dutton. Take care on the lane, which is narrow. The nursery has a large car park where they are very happy to accommodate walkers, but you should check the website for opening times: www.bluebellcottage.co.uk. **Sat Nav:** WA4 4HP. Alternatively, there is parking at the Leigh Arms for patrons or in the lane alongside for others. **Sat Nav:** CW8 4QT.

Refreshments The Bluebell Cottage tea room serves hot and cold drinks, wonderful home-made cakes and Cheshire ice cream ☎ 01928 713718 www.bluebellcottage.co.uk. The Leigh Arms serves food all day at weekends, and at lunchtimes and in the evening during the week ☎ 01606 853327 www.leigharms.co.uk.

The Walk

1 From the Bluebell Cottage Gardens and Nursery car park, cross the wild flower meadow at the end to enter the bluebell wood. An obvious circular path will bring you out to the meadow again, and you can then continue down to the road. Opposite the entrance gate, a signpost directs you into a deep wooded valley spread with bluebells and wood anemones. Follow the path that runs above the stream, soon crossing it to emerge finally on a broad track.

2 Turn left on the track, keep right at the fork, and immediately take a cross-field path on the left, signed as the **Delamere Way**. Go through a gate into **Dutton Park**, owned by the Woodland Trust, where more bluebells gild the bank on your right. Pass a small lake, and continue to the very obvious bridge vaulting the **River Weaver**. Over on your right, you can see **Dutton Viaduct**, carrying the railway over the Weaver Valley. Built in 1836, it is one of the earliest of its kind, and a Grade II* listed building.

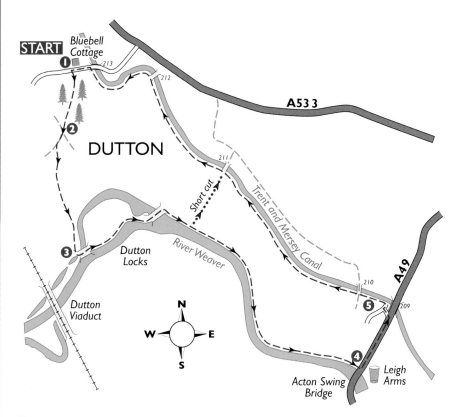

3 Turn left to cross the bridge. You are now on an island; the water channel beside you was created to take boats through the **Dutton Locks** ahead, where boats negotiate a difference in level of eight feet. On the far side of the locks is a mooring for small craft, and beyond that, the sad skeleton of *Chica*, once a hotel boat, who sits half-submerged in the water. Keep ahead to cross another bridge over the Weaver with the sluice gate downstream. Continue on the tarmacked track beside the river for 100 metres or so to a signpost pointing through fields on the left. This is the shortcut, taking you directly to Bridge 211 (see Point 5). For the longer walk, simply continue beside the river for another mile to reach the **Acton Swing Bridge**, which carries the A49. The Weaver is navigable for twenty miles, from Winsford to its junction with the Manchester Ship Canal. Although once important for carrying salt and coal, commercial traffic has now virtually ceased. Acton Swing Bridge is a reminder of the large craft that once plied these waters.

4 The **Leigh Arms**, opposite you now, is the alternative starting point for this walk. Turn left here, keeping to the pavement alongside the road. After about

Dutton Locks with the viaduct in the background.

a quarter of a mile, a road dips down on the left, signposted to **Davenports Tea Room**. Go down this road, keeping to the right, and go through the **Black Prince** boatyard to reach the canal towpath.

5 Turn left now, and simply follow the canal. At Bridge 211, the shortcut joins, and from here you have almost a mile of most pleasant waterside walking, with some splendid views to the south, before you reach the Bridge 213 (a brick bridge). Leave the canal here, turning left down **Lodge Lane** to return to **Bluebell Cottage**.

What to look out for –

Bluebell Cottage

There's so much on this walk: wild flowers everywhere, locks on the River Weaver, boats on the Trent and Mersey Canal. And Bluebell Cottage itself is more than worth a visit. Entry to the nursery, tea room and bluebell wood is free; there is a small charge for the garden itself. Allow yourself time – this is a real gem!

In Bluebell Cottage gardens.

If you have enjoyed this walk

Just about all the woods in the Weaver Valley are rich in bluebells. Try Warburton's Wood or Hunter's Wood near Kingsley, both owned by the Cheshire Wildlife Trust. And if you want to see more of the River Weaver, the Weaver Way follows it from Audlem to Frodsham, a distance of 40 miles.

spring

Looking _____ _____ Audlem.

3 *Audlem*

6 miles (9.6 km)

May is surely the month for boating! Maybe it's because there's some expectation of better weather after the long winter; or maybe it's because boat hire is less expensive than in high summer: but those waterways enthusiasts are out in their droves. And where better to see them than at Audlem? Here, fifteen locks in close succession take the Shropshire Union Canal from the plains of Cheshire to the relative heights of the Midlands. The Audlem fifteen remain as demanding as ever for boaters, and you can have some fun as an observer, but before that you have a pleasant little ramble through the surrounding countryside, taking in a picturesque old mill on the infant River Weaver. When you return to the wharf, you should definitely take a look in the canal shop, an Aladdin's cave known as Audlem Mill. This walk could easily be divided into two circuits of 3½ and 2½ miles respectively.

The Facts

Terrain Canal towpath, field paths, quiet lanes.

Map OS Explorer 257 Crewe & Nantwich.

Starting point The main car park in the centre of Audlem (GR SJ 659437).

How to get there & parking Audlem is on the A525 Whitchurch–Newcastle road. In the centre of Audlem, keep the church on your right to go up Cheshire Street. The free car park is on your left. **Sat Nav:** CW3 0AH.

Refreshments There's quite a choice in Audlem, but surely the most appropriate venue is the Shroppie Fly on the wharf, with its boat-shaped bar. If it's a nice day, you could sit at the outside tables surveying the watery scene ☎ 01270 812379 www.shroppiefly.com. Also worth a visit is Audlem Mill, which sells Snugburys' delicious ice cream.

The Walk

❶ From the car park, cross the playing field to take a path at the far left-hand corner leading down to **Audlem Wharf**. Here, turn right (with the canal on your left) and walk down past the lowest three locks and on along the towpath. Continue for about a mile, crossing a short aqueduct over the **River Weaver** and passing the entrance to **Overwater Marina** to reach Bridge 80. Note the metal guards on the sides of the bridge, which have been deeply gouged by the ropes of horse-drawn barges.

❷ Go under the bridge, and turn right to go up stone steps to a rough lane. Turn left, and in about 100 metres, look for a metal gate into a field on the right. Go through this, and cross the field, angling slightly right to a stile. Cross the track to another stile, and continue on the clearly marked path alongside the hedge to reach a tarmacked lane. The lane soon descends to old **Hankelow Mill**, now converted into desirable residences. Keep ahead on the lane, with a wooded valley to your right, to emerge at the main road.

❸ The road does have verges, but take care here. Turn left, and about fifty metres up, on the opposite side (just past the big farm entrance), a gate admits you to a field path. Walk up the field with the hedge on your right, and at the top corner, enter a strip of woodland through a kissing gate. A narrow path now leads through the trees beside a big house (**the Parkes**) and brings you onto its

Spring

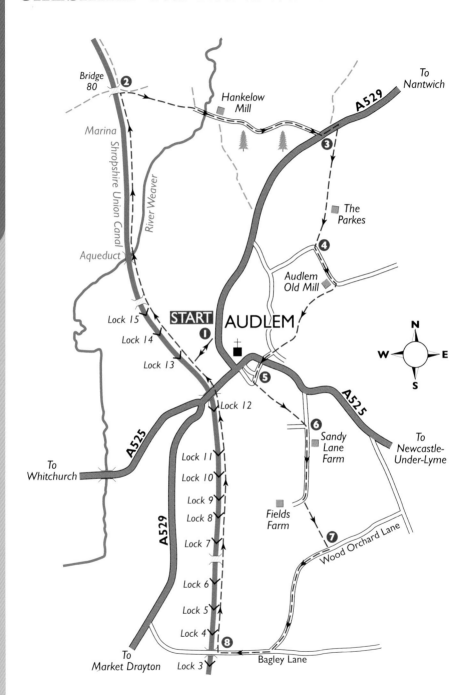

Bridge
80 ❷

To
Nantwich

Hankelow
Mill

A529

Marina

Shropshire Union Canal

River Weaver

❸

The
Parkes

Aqueduct

❹

Audlem
Old Mill

Lock 15

Lock 14

START
❶

AUDLEM

Lock 13

❺

N
W — E
S

Lock 12

A525

A525

To
Newcastle-
Under-Lyme

❻

Sandy
Lane
Farm

To
Whitchurch

Lock 11

Lock 10

Lock 9

Fields
Farm

Lock 8

A529

Lock 7

❼

Wood Orchard Lane

Lock 6

Lock 5

Lock 4

❽

To
Market Drayton

Lock 3

Bagley Lane

spring

The wharf at Audlem.

access road. Keep ahead to arrive at a lane.

4 Turn left here, and continue for 300 metres to a house (**Audlem Old Mill**). Here, take a bridleway on the right – a pleasant track between high hedges that eventually reaches dwellings on the outskirts of Audlem. At the tarmacked road, go left (not sharp left) to meet the A525. Cross straight over to continue down **School Lane**.

5 At the first junction, you have the possibility of a shortcut. Turning right up **Vicarage Lane** will take you straight back to the church, and you can walk around it to find the car park. To continue with the walk, keep left at this junction, passing in front of a house. At the small green with picnic tables, turn left to cross the stream, then continue on the clear path uphill and across the field.

6 A stile takes you to a tarmacked farm access road at **Sandy Lane Farm**. Ignore the track on your right here, and maintain the same direction to pass between the farmhouse and some sheds. Where the road swings right to **Fields Farm**, keep ahead on the earthen track to reach quiet **Wood Orchard Lane**.

7 Turn right, and continue to a road junction in about three quarters of a mile. Here, turn right on **Bagley Lane**, and in about 400 metres, reach a bridge over the canal.

8 At this bridge, Lock 3 is on your left. Go down to the canal beside it, and turn right. Now, you can simply walk down beside the long flight of locks, enjoying the activity all the way back to Audlem Wharf.

What to look out for –

Audlem Locks

You should have plenty of opportunity to figure out the working of a lock! Simply a chamber containing water, the lock is filled by opening paddles at the top gate, and emptied via paddles at the bottom. Simple? Well, yes – but there's lots of potential for getting it wrong. Open both sets of paddles at once and you get nowhere,

Approaching Lock 4.

because the water just rushes through. It does happen – usually because the previous boat has left a paddle open and no one has noticed.

If you have enjoyed this walk

Does Cheshire have more canals than any other county in England? There don't seem to be any statistics, but certainly fourteen different canals pass through it, so there's plenty of choice for waterways enthusiasts. Try Walks 4, 8 and 12 for a start.

spring

The Salt Line in early spring.

4 *The Salt Line*
6 or 5 miles (9.6 or 8 km)

In Britain's gardens, spring arrives with a flourish. Suddenly there are bright daffodils, pink cherry blossom, golden forsythia and multicoloured primulas. The countryside is rather more subtle about things: green dog's mercury on the woodland floor, white splashes of blackthorn blossom in the hedgerows, new green leaves on the hawthorns, and celandines and coltsfoot appearing on the banks.

Take this walk in March to enjoy all the early manifestations of spring. The route begins on the Salt Line, the restored trackbed of a railway that once carried salt from Nantwich and Middlewich to the Potteries. Cheshire East Council now looks after the Salt Line, and there are display boards detailing wildlife, a tree information trail (pick up a free leaflet in the car park), a nature reserve, and a bench or picnic table every 400 metres. Posts have also been placed along the two-mile length of the Salt Line showing the universe to scale, so you can even see how far away Neptune is from Earth.

The return along the Trent and Mersey Canal promises yet more interest, with narrowboats on the move through no fewer than five locks along this short stretch. Omitting the walk around Borrow Pit Meadows will reduce this walk to five miles (eight km).

CHESHIRE Year Round Walks

Terrain Hard-surfaced track, lane, canal towpath.

Map OS Explorer 268 Wilmslow, Macclesfield & Congleton.

Starting point Salt Line and Borrow Pit Meadows car park (GR SJ 775582).

How to get there & parking From the A533, turn south, signposted to Hassall Green. Continue through the village; the car park is on the right, just after passing under the motorway. **Sat Nav:** CW11 4YB.

Refreshments There are picnic tables along the length of the Salt Line and again at Rode Heath Rise. The nearest inn is probably the Horseshoe, which you will pass on the walk at the junction on Cherry Lane. Everything from lunchtime snacks to Sunday roasts feature on the extensive menu ☎ 01270 876070 www.horseshoeinn.co.uk.

The Walk _____

❶ Before you leave the car park, walk down to the overflow car park to locate the **Sun** in the corner. Mercury, Venus and Earth are surprisingly close. You can pick up a leaflet for the tree trail at this point, too. Then cross the road and simply follow the **Salt Line**, crossing over a very minor road at one point.

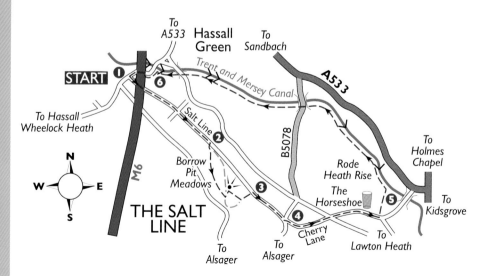

Cherry Lane near point 4.

2 After about a mile, turn right, following the tree trail signs, into the nature reserve of **Borrow Pit Meadows**. (This is an optional part of the walk; if you carry on along the Salt Line you will quickly come to Point 3.) After entering Borrow Pit Meadows, the tree trail signs direct you right at the first junction. Continue now round the big field to a T-junction of paths. Go left here to a viewpoint over the lake, then keep right, going downhill to a junction of many paths. The lake is now on your left, and it is possible to walk right round it if you wish. Otherwise, keep ahead, uphill, and you will soon meet the Salt Line again.

3 Turn right, and follow the Salt Line to its end at a road.

4 Cross the road diagonally to continue up **Cherry Lane**, with a residential area on your left. At the crossroads in about 300 metres, cross straight over, and keep ahead for about 400 metres to where **Lawton Heath Lane** comes in from the right. On the left here, a track is signposted to a kennels and cattery. Take this, and continue past the kennels, over the brook and up the hill to the canal.

5 You are now at **Rode Heath Rise**, the site of a one-time salt works and now a nature reserve. Turn left, and continue along the towpath of the **Trent and Mersey Canal**. Almost immediately you will reach a lock. Boaters call this particular section of the canal **Heartbreak Hill**, because there are twenty-six locks in seven miles, and it can take all day to get through them. The canal was opened in 1777, but half a century later it was so busy and congested that Thomas Telford, the famous engineer, was called in for advice. One of his solutions was to double the locks so that two boats could use them at a time. Some of these parallel locks have since been filled in, but the second lock on this walk still has both chambers functioning.

6 In about two miles, at the fifth lock, go under the bridge and then left up to the road. Go right on the road (not over the canal), and with great care, walk down the road and under the motorway to reach the car park.

What to look out for –

Information boards

There's so much! Trees on the tree trail, wild flowers in Borrow Pit Meadows (a board details all you can find), planets on the solar system trail, boats and locks on the canal. Spring is a wonderful time to take this walk – but with so much here, surely, it's a walk for all seasons.

If you have enjoyed this walk

There are many restored railway lines in Cheshire – though maybe none so packed with interest as the Salt Line. See Walk 18 for more ideas. And if you particularly enjoyed the canal, Cheshire's not short on those either. To do things in style, you could explore the whole county by walking the Cheshire Ring, ninety-seven miles of towpath along six different canals. It can be done!

Tegg's Nose Reservoir.

5 *Macclesfield Forest*
6 or 4½ miles (9.6 or 7.2 km)

Think spring, think bird nesting time! Nests aren't usually that easy to spot, though, because their owners have them well hidden away. Here, however, at Trentabank Reservoir in Macclesfield Forest, there are some nests that are more than obvious: the huge, grey, twiggy masses of a heronry. Doesn't it seem curious that birds as big and heavy as herons should choose to nest in the swaying treetops? Of course, the trees are always near water, where the herons find much of their food. The heronry at Trentabank is occupied for four or five months of the year, and there's a perfectly placed viewing area, so bring your binoculars along and there should be plenty to see.

Macclesfield Forest also offers a splendid variety of waymarked walks. The route here is an amalgamation of these, taking in the Forest Chapel, four reservoirs and a really magnificent balcony path with views of Cheshire's highest moorland.

spring

The Facts

Terrain Forest paths and stony tracks. If you thought Cheshire was a flat county, this walk will make you think again!

Map OS Explorer OL24 The Peak District.

Starting point Macclesfield Forest Visitor Centre (GR SJ 962712).

How to get there & parking From the A523, a mile south of Macclesfield, follow signs to Langley. In the village, follow signs to Macclesfield Forest, keeping right at the Leather's Smithy pub, then keeping left at the next junction to park in the pay and display car park. Alternatively, there is some free designated roadside parking close to the entrance. **Sat Nav:** SK11 0NS.

Refreshments The Forest Snug, a mobile van selling sandwiches, home-made cakes, ice creams and the like, parks at the visitor centre at weekends all year round (from around 10 a.m. until 4 p.m.) and on Tuesdays and Wednesdays in summer. For more substantial fare, there's the Leather's Smithy pub, near Point 7 ☎ 01260 252313 www.leatherssmithy.co.uk.

The Walk _____

❶ Leaving the visitor centre, turn right on the road; in about 200 metres, you will reach the heronry viewpoint with its information panel. The heronry is clearly visible across the water, but you will see a lot more with binoculars. When ready to leave, take the path opposite the viewpoint, doubling back towards the visitor centre. In a few metres, turn sharp left (signposted to **Shutlingsloe**), and at the next junction, keep straight ahead on a path parallel to, and above, the road. This path now dodges through woodland, always with the road in sight, until eventually it runs beside a stone wall and reaches a gap onto the road.

❷ Cross the road to a path opposite, bending right and climbing steadily before dipping to meet a forest track. Turn left here (signposted to **Forest Chapel**), and climb more steeply. At the forest edge, a track joins from the right, and from here you have red-banded posts to take you as far as Point 4. Continue climbing ahead, then turn right on reaching a lane to arrive at Forest Chapel. The 17th-century Church of St Stephen, known as Forest Chapel, is probably more notable for its remote hillside setting than its architecture. In mid-August, the church stages an ancient rush-bearing ceremony, it which fresh rushes are strewn on the floor and plaited for decorations.

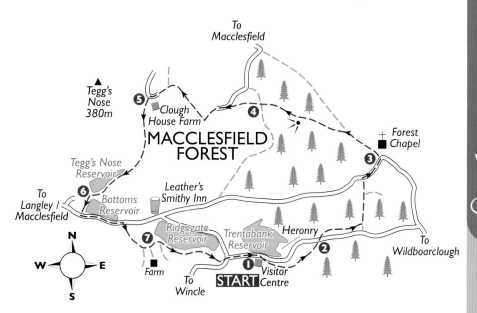

3 Turn left here, and walk uphill on a walled, stony lane. Look back as you go, to see the **Cat and Fiddle Moors** (named after an old pub) across the valley, with the Buxton road winding its way across them. To the left is Shining Tor, Cheshire's highest point at 559 metres. After about 300 metres, take a path branching left into the forest, confirmed by a red-banded post. Continue on this lovely path for almost a mile before dropping to a forest road. Where the forest has been cleared there are wide-ranging views. Behind you is the distinctive shape of Shutlingsloe (506 metres), while ahead the land falls away to the Cheshire Plain.

4 At this junction, the red-marked trail turns left, and offers a shortcut to Point 7. To continue with the main route, cross straight over to take the path alongside the ruined barn, signposted to **Tegg's Nose**, a craggy hill (380 metres) that will soon appear ahead. Very soon you emerge on a road. Turn left, and walk downhill past the house, after which the road becomes a narrow, stony lane. The lane soon turns right (you could cut this corner on a cross-field path), and then continues its rocky descent for a further 600 metres before crossing a stream, bending left and becoming tarmacked. Continue to the junction above **Clough House Farm**.

5 Turn left, passing through a gate onto a path signposted as Tegg's Nose

spring

Macclesfield Forest

Trail. In half a mile or so, you reach **Tegg's Nose Reservoir** and then the dam at its far end.

6 Turn left here to cross the dam on **Bottoms Reservoir**, and bear left alongside it to emerge on the road. Continue up the road. Should you feel in need of resuscitation, the **Leather's Smithy** pub is straight ahead of you here. Just after the end of the reservoir, take a track on the right (signposted as **Gritstone Trail**). Cross a cattle grid, then fork left towards the farm. After about 100 metres, a gate on the left admits you to the woodland, and you can climb to the rim of **Ridgegate Reservoir**.

7 Turn right, and after crossing the end of the reservoir, keep left at the fork. Continue through the woods above the reservoir to finally descend and bend left to a road junction. Cross to the road opposite (signposted to **Forest Chapel**) to return to the visitor centre.

What to look out for –

Trentabank Heronry

With around twenty nests, Trentabank is the largest heronry in the Peak District. The birds return year after year to the same nests. Eggs are laid in March, and take around a month to hatch; the young have generally flown by July.

If you have enjoyed this walk

Cheshire's biggest heronry (and possibly the biggest in the UK) is on the north side of Budworth Mere, near Marbury Country Park. The heronry itself is on private land, but you can visit the mere. If more forest walks appeal, pick up a leaflet showing the marked routes from the board outside the visitor centre.

Walking across to Middle Eye from Little Eye.

Hilbre Island

4 miles (6.4 km)

At the mouth of the Dee Estuary, Hilbre Island and its lesser siblings Middle Eye and Little Eye are accessible for about three hours on either side of low tide. Little Eye is no more than a big tuft of grass, and Middle Eye a raised grassy plateau, but Hilbre, the largest and farthest out, has a little more to offer: a few private houses, an old telegraph station and a crumbling lifeboat station, but still no electricity or running water, and no full-time inhabitants. On a sunny summer's day, the journey across the sands to these islands is popular, so is not one you'll be making alone, but even so there is something of an adventure about it.

Naturally, an island like Hilbre has its history. The name derives from St Hildeburgh, who was thought to have lived here in the seventh century. Later it had its own Benedictine monastery, and in the Middle Ages it was a major coastal trading point. Today, with the estuary silted up, Hilbre is important for its wildlife. Gulls of all kinds bob on the shallow waters; oyster catchers, dunlins, curlews, shelducks and many more squabble and feed at the tidal margin. Then there are the grey seals that gather on a sandbank to the west of the island; they can usually be seen cavorting in the waters off its tip. Don't forget your binoculars!

Terrain Firm sand and rock. Some sections may be wet underfoot, so choose your footwear accordingly.

Map Hilbre appears on OS Explorer 266 Wirral & Chester, but the map isn't especially useful for this walk. Better to follow the directions and map here.

Starting point North end of Marine Lake, West Kirby (GR SJ 210867).

How to get there & parking In West Kirby, follow the brown signs to Marine Lake. You can find a pay and display car park by turning into the Morrisons entrance and immediately branching right. There is free parking on the seafront opposite, but it may be difficult to find a space. **Sat Nav:** CH48 0QA.

Refreshments The kiosk beside the car park sells hot and cold drinks, ice cream and simple hot food such as burgers and fish and chips. There are plenty of other options in West Kirby though. Note that there are no services or water on the island (although there is a composting toilet).

The Walk

If you are planning this walk, be sure to check the tide tables first (**www.tidetimes. org.uk/hilbre-island-tide-times**). *Official advice is that you* **must** *leave Hilbre at least three hours before high tide, or earlier if you walk slowly.*

On no account *should you try to shortcut across the sands between Hilbre and West Kirby, either on the way out or on the way back. There are deep pools and water channels. The route described is the only safe way to reach Hilbre.*

❶ From the north end of **Marine Lake**, beside the toilets, walk down the slipway onto the sand. You should clearly see the three islands. Walk straight out across the sand, aiming for the left side of the nearest island, **Little Eye**.

❷ Reaching Little Eye, take the official route, which is to walk round on the red rocks behind it, bearing right to cross half a mile of sand to **Middle Eye**. Note: Middle Eye is called **Little Hilbre** on the OS map. Now keep Middle Eye on your left, and continue over more rocks to its north end. Or you can walk over the top of Middle Eye if you prefer.

❸ **Hilbre** is very close at this point. Pick your way across rock, aiming for the

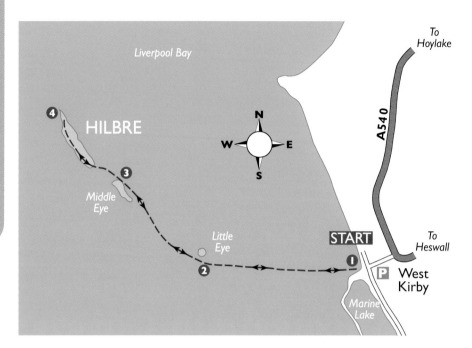

left-hand side of the island, where a firm track leads uphill. Follow this to pass the former telegraph station, and then leave the track to reach the old lifeboat station at the tip.

4 When you have had a good look around the island, you simply need to return the way you came – not forgetting to take note of the tide times!

A house on Hilbre Island.

What to look out for –

Birds and seals

The birds on Hilbre are something quite special. The first building you see on reaching the island is a bird observatory, which is manned most days. And who can resist the seals? The Friends of Hilbre have open days when they offer the public the opportunity to view them with their telescope. See www.hilbreisland.info for details.

If you have enjoyed this walk

There are apparently forty-three unbridged tidal islands around the UK. If you are looking for another similar adventure, the nearest of these is probably Llanddwyn Island on Anglesey, some eighty miles away. But if it's the seabirds that have captured your attention, try Walk 16 at Parkgate – or indeed anywhere on the shores of the Dee Estuary.

summer

Views from Bickerton Hill.

Bickerton Hill

4½ miles (7.2 km)

A long ridge of sandstone extends south from the Mersey Estuary into the heart of Cheshire. Along its length are strange rocky outcrops, curious caves and thick oak woodland, but surely the best is kept till last, the southernmost hill at Bickerton.

Bickerton Hill is a rare landscape of lowland heath, a Site of Special Scientific Interest that is now under the care of the National Trust. Nothing could be more glorious than standing at its summit on a sunny August day, purple heather blazing at your feet and all the country between the Shropshire Hills and the Mersey Estuary spread before you.

Lowland heath supports a variety of unusual plant and animal life, and on a warm day you might just spot a lizard, a grass snake or a slow-worm here. If you come in August, you certainly will encounter the purple ling heather; come earlier, and the brighter bell heather will be at its best; or later, and the bilberries that clothe the ground will be wearing autumn shades of red. Yellow gorse and white-trunked silver birch add yet more colour to the scene.

On this walk, there should be plenty of time to take it all in as you traverse the length of the hill, visit the Iron Age fort at its summit, and then return through the pretty village of Brown Knowl, crouching beneath the slopes.

Terrain Rocky and sandy footpaths with some steps; minor lanes.

Map OS Explorer 257 Crewe & Nantwich.

Starting point National Trust car park, Bickerton (GR SJ 503531).

How to get there & parking Travelling west on the A534 Nantwich–Wrexham road, a mile after passing through Bulkeley, turn left where signposted to Bickerton. At the church, go straight over into Goldford Lane, then in half a mile, turn right alongside a pond, going up a rough track bearing a National Trust sign. After about 200 metres, you reach a large parking area. **Sat Nav:** SY14 8LN.

Refreshments None on the walk. The nearest is the very welcoming Bickerton Poacher, SY14 8BE, two miles north-east ☎ 01829 720226 www.bickertonpoacher.co.uk. Alternatively, try the Egerton Arms, CH3 9JW, three miles north-west ☎ 01829 782241 www.egerton-arms.com.

The Walk

❶ Leave the car park through the wooden gate, and walk gently uphill. At the fork in 200 metres, go left, then keep ahead at the cross-tracks to climb stone steps, following the footprint sign of the **Sandstone Trail**. Continue along the obvious path, rising steadily to the hill fort at the summit (212 metres). On its far side, steps lead down to an information panel. Maiden Castle hill fort was built around 600 BC. The heathland was probably as it is today: an area of forest cleared and kept low by the grazing animals of those who lived here. Sadly, little of significance has been found on excavation.

❷ Keep straight ahead now. (Do not turn down the steep slope with the Sandstone Trail.) The path soon passes through a gate, entering a wood of silver birch. Bear right with the path to descend to a junction above a steep slope. Turn left here, and after a few ups and downs you are on a path dipping firmly downhill. At a T-junction, double back to the right, and continue to descend through the wood until you meet a path at the bottom of the hill. This is again the Sandstone Trail, and following it right along the wall, then left and left again, will bring you to **Duckington car park** on your right.

❸ Turn right, going through the car park and then uphill again through another gate. Keep ahead at a junction; the path becomes narrower, and soon dips to a clearing with an information panel. Go through the wooden gate

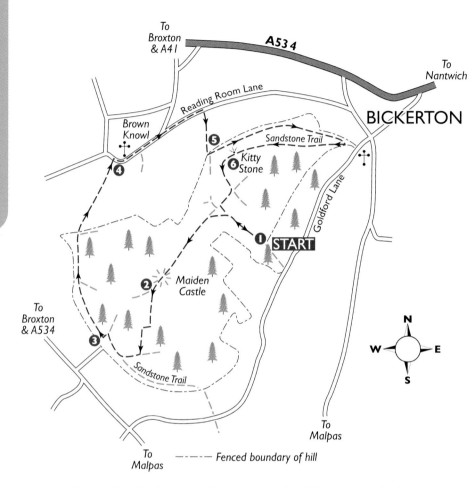

here, and keep directly ahead on the broad track, which eventually becomes a tarmacked lane in the village of **Brown Knowl**.

④ Reaching the end of the lane, turn right, and follow the road as it bends to the left. On your left, now, is **Brown Knowl Methodist Church**, a Grade II listed building which was built on the site of a former Primitive Methodist chapel. Continue down the pretty village street, bearing right at the bottom into **Reading Room Lane**. In about 300 metres, opposite a red-brick house, look for a stile in the hedge. Cross this, and climb along the field edge to enter the National Trust land again.

⑤ Now go left, following the fence along the bottom of the hill. At length,

summer

The main street in the pretty village of Brown Knowl.

the path cuts a corner, and begins to climb steeply to reach a junction with a wooden gate over to the left. Turn right here; you are now once again on the Sandstone Trail. The broad path continues uphill, going up a few steps and later passing a rocky overhang, before the final rise to the **Kitty Stone**. This is a poignant memorial to the wife of the benefactor who enabled the National Trust to purchase this land.

⑥ The path bears left now and descends. Follow the Sandstone Trail signs to reach a junction near an information panel. Go right here down a sunken track; then, very soon, turn left to return down the broad track to the car park.

What to look out for –

The view

The view from Maiden Castle: on your right and quite close is Raw Head, at 227 metres the highest point of the Peckforton Hills. Just left of that, you can see the Mersey Estuary and the Wirral; on a clear day, you should be able to pick out both Liverpool and Chester Cathedrals (binoculars help!). Left again are the Clwydian Hills, then the high Berwyns, followed by the strange humps that are the volcanic Breiddens. Still further left, and very far away, rise the 'blue remembered hills' of Shropshire.

If you have enjoyed this walk

There's more heather-clad lowland heath at Thurstaston Common on the Wirral Peninsula, with some splendid views across the Dee Estuary thrown in. For the same landscape without the views, try Little Budworth Country Park, about ten miles north-east from Bickerton. And for more about the Sandstone Trail, see Walk 1.

Looking down Hurleston locks.

Hurleston

6 miles (9.6 km)

Starting at Hurleston, where the Llangollen and Shropshire Union Canals meet, this walk is almost entirely on canal towpaths. The junction itself is a fascinating place. The Llangollen Canal is thirty-four feet above the Shropshire Union, so boats travelling between the two must pass through four very deep locks. The locks aren't in a staircase, but there is very little room between them, so some careful navigating is required of the boaters. On a busy day, it can be an interesting spectacle!

From Hurleston, the Shropshire Union Canal meanders south to the village of Acton, where an information panel points out the scene of a Civil War battle in 1644. The nearby church bears the scars of musket balls from that day. A short trip across the fields follows, and you can simply amble home along the canal. And why take this walk in summer? Because just a short distance along the road from your parked car is Snugburys Ice Cream, where the absolutely delicious home-made ice-cream comes in around forty different varieties. Once the difficult choice is made, you can enjoy it from a seat in the flower-filled courtyard, or stroll into the field to admire the latest hay sculpture. Snugburys creates a new one every year!

The Facts

summer

Terrain Canal towpath and cross-field paths.

Map OS Explorer 257 Crewe & Nantwich.

Starting point Parking area off the A51 at Hurleston Bridge (GR 621551).

How to get there & parking From Nantwich, take the B5341 north in the direction of Barbridge. After passing through the village of Acton, continue for a mile and a half, joining the A51 towards Barbridge on the way. The parking area is on the left, immediately before the canal bridge, and is signed as a no through road. **Sat Nav:** CW5 6BU.

Refreshments Ice cream, of course! Snugburys is about 400 metres south down the A51. Take your car, or on foot, cross the road with care to the pavement opposite, then cross back to the wide verge. Snugburys offers a range of hot drinks and a limited choice of cake and biscuits ☎ 01270 624830 www.snugburys.co.uk.

The Walk

1 Leave the parking area at the top corner, go down the steps to the canal towpath, and turn right to reach the lock flight. Walk down beside it, and after crossing the bridge at the bottom, turn right along the towpath.

2 Continue on the towpath for a mile and a half to Bridge 93, **Acton Bridge**, and climb the steps. A display panel details the Parliamentarian victory here in

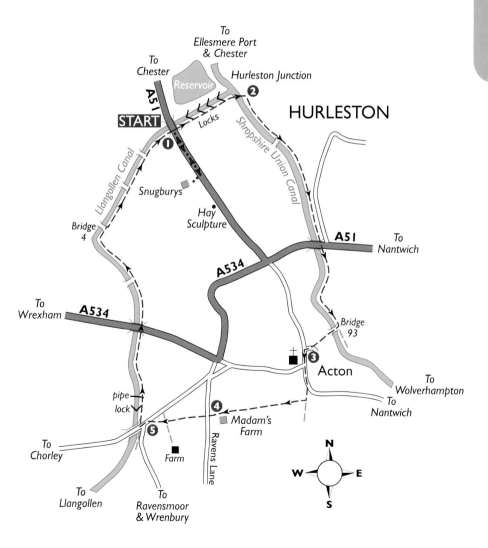

Bridge 4 on the Llangollen Canal.

January 1644, and shows the positions of the armies. Continue across Acton Bridge and up the path through the crop field to come out between houses. Turn right now to walk up to the main road.

③ Turn left on the main road. **Acton Church** is almost opposite you here, and you may want to scan its south side, where pockmarks from the musket balls can be seen. The church was initially a Royalist stronghold, but was taken by the Parliamentarians and used to house their prisoners. Continue along the main road, passing the derelict **Star Inn**. About fifty metres after this, keep ahead on the track signposted to **Dorfold Farm**. Do not cross the cattle grid, but take a path on the right just before it, and walk along the edge of the field. Cross the next crop field directly to emerge at a strip of wasteland. Two waymarked posts lead you through this to cross another field. Now a stile points you alongside the garden of **Madam's Farm** and down its access road to reach a lane.

④ Cross the lane to the path opposite, and walk straight across the field, passing a huge oak tree. Two more oaks in the far hedge mark the gap into a second field, in which you should maintain the same direction. After crossing a private access road, bear diagonally right in the final field to come out on a lane. Turn left, ignore the left turn at the junction, and look for the steps on the left before the canal bridge.

⑤ Once down beside the canal, turn right to pass under the bridge, and continue past a lock, then under several bridges, until after about 1½ miles you gain access to your car beside Bridge 1.

What to look out for –

Narrowboats

Narrowboats are always interesting; you may well see one with 'Roses and Castles' painting, highly polished brassware and decorative lace in the back cabin. 19th-century working boat people liked to brighten up their lives with these classic embellishments, and some present-day boaters keep up the tradition.

'Roses and Castles' painting.

If you have enjoyed this walk

There are so many canal walks in Cheshire! Have a look at Walks 2, 3 and 19 in this book, or think big, and take on the ninety-seven miles of the Cheshire Ring. See en.wikipedia.org/wiki/Cheshire_Ring.

summer

View across the Dane valley from the arboretum.

Swettenham

4 or 2 miles (6.4 or 3.2 km)

Think summer, think flowers: gardens bursting with colour, and wild flowers in the meadows and hedgerows. The little village of Swettenham, in the Dane Valley, surely captures the essence of summer, its old pub garlanded with bright blooms, and beyond it, a field planted with lavender.

In contrast to all this are the wild flower meadows beside the nearby river, managed by the Cheshire Wildlife Trust. Here the going is rougher underfoot, and the flowers perhaps less showy, but meadowsweet, red campion and bird's-foot trefoil, among others, have huge appeal for the butterflies.

Two separate short circuits from Swettenham take in the meadows, but the village has yet another treat in store. For more than sixty years, the big house beside the pub was home to Sir Bernard Lovell, who was responsible for the planting of a thirty-acre arboretum. This beautiful and fascinating garden could offer an hour or two of walking in itself, but in following the second of these circuits, you will see the best of it, an avenue of native trees and some remarkable shrubs beside a lake deep in the valley.

The Facts

summer

Terrain Lanes, rough field paths, and grassy tracks in the arboretum.

Map OS Explorer 268 Wilmslow, Macclesfield & Congleton.

Starting point The Swettenham Arms pub car park (GR SJ 799671).

How to get there & parking From Holmes Chapel, take the A535 north in the direction of Macclesfield, and in about two miles, in the village of Twemlow Green, turn right where signposted to Swettenham. Keep following the signs. The huge car parking area is alongside the inn and church in the centre of the village. Swettenham can also be reached from the A54 east of Congleton. **Sat Nav:** CW12 2LF.

Refreshments Very imaginative food is served all day, every day at the Swettenham Arms ☎ 01477 571284 www.swettenhamarms.co.uk.

The Walk

First circuit

1 From the car park exit, a signed path on the left leads into the lavender field. Turn right alongside the hedge, and continue to the far corner of the field, where a short path leads down to a lane. Walk right for about twenty metres to find a path on the left leading down into the valley. The path traverses a bridge over **Swettenham Brook** and climbs to a path junction.

2 Turn right here, winding through thick vegetation to emerge on a hard-surfaced farm track. Go right on this track, and in a few minutes, you will see a gate into the nature reserve. Do not go through this gate, but keep ahead, passing a large house to reach a second gate, which is set back on the right.

3 Go through this gate into the **Swettenham Meadows Nature Reserve**. If the grass is high, the path may not be obvious, but walk straight across the field until you can see the fence edging the woodland. Now go right until you meet a wooden gate in that fence. Through this gate, the path is clearer, and you can follow it over rough ground and a couple of boardwalks before reaching another gate. A few metres further on is the gate you passed by earlier. The small Dexter cattle that sometimes graze here keep the grass short while leaving the wild flowers. They are very good-natured and will ignore visitors, but taking dogs near cattle can never be recommended.

4 Do not go through the gate; instead, go sharp left down the slope, passing

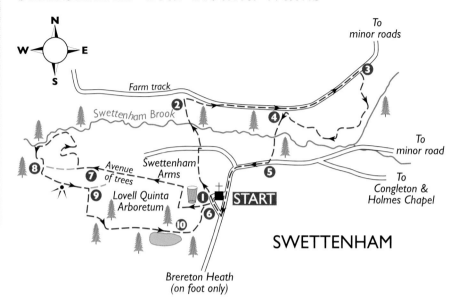

over a couple of wooden bridges and descending some steps to the brook. Cross the bridge here, and continue up the far side to meet the lane.

⑤ Turn right here, then bear left at the corner to return to the church, and behind it, the car park.

Second circuit

⑥ Now leave the car park via the gate into the **Lovell Quinta Arboretum**, to the left of the inn. The arboretum is now maintained by the Tatton Garden Society, and an honesty box requests a donation towards its upkeep. Through the entrance gate, bear sharply right, and after walking a short path through the trees, you will see an avenue of native trees on your left. Walk down through the avenue to the gate at its end.

⑦ Go through the gate, here entering the nature reserve, and continue for 100 metres or so, where a path leads off on the right. Follow this to go through another gate, then go immediately right through yet another gate into a lovely sloping field. Here, a clear path winds down to **Swettenham Brook**, then continues alongside it. Eventually, a classical sequence of thirty-nine steps takes you out of the valley to leave the reserve.

⑧ At the exit gate, go right to skirt the woodland and arrive at another small wooden gate. Through this, a fenced path along the top of a field gives sweeping views across the valley of the River Dane.

9 Leave the fenced path through a gate; you are now in the arboretum again. Keep straight ahead past Post 13 to reach a seat on a corner beside a clearing. Turn left here, passing a superb Lebanon oak on your right at the corner. Shortly, with Post 11 about fifteen metres ahead, bear right between two big conifers. Pass Post 10 and Post 9, veer slightly right past Posts 8, 7 and 6, and keep straight on, alongside the lake.

The Swettenham Arms.

10 At the top of the lake, continue into the clearing ahead and bear left. The trees here are all 'silver', and were planted to commemorate Sir Bernard and Lady Lovell's twenty-fifth wedding anniversary. Exit the clearing by Post 3, then pass Post 2, and bear right to Post 1 near the gate leading into the car park.

What to look out for –

Butterflies

On a sunny day, look out for the butterflies in the meadow – brimstone, orange tip and meadow brown, for a start, but there are many more. And if you want to identify some of the trees in the arboretum, pick up a laminated walk guide on the right as you enter.

Meadow Brown butterfly.

If you have enjoyed this walk

The Cheshire Wildlife Trust cares for many more nature reserves across the county. Go to their website: www.cheshirewildlifetrust.org.uk.

View coming down from Shutlingsloe.

Shutlingsloe

4 miles (6.4 km)

When asked why he wanted to climb Everest, George Mallory famously replied, 'because it's there'. At 506 metres, Shutlingsloe isn't even a mountain, but it's certainly a very curiously shaped hill, and when you see something like that, you just have to scale it for the same reason that Mallory gave. And of course, you can tell the view from the top will be stunning!

Shutlingsloe has been dubbed 'Cheshire's Matterhorn', presumably because, with abundant imagination, its steep-sided summit could be thought to bear a humble resemblance to the distant giant. For sure, the final part of the ascent here is abrupt, with many rough-hewn steps, but the earlier climb from the valley of the Clough Brook is gentle enough, and the return route through that valley is a delightful path in itself.

In August, the lower slopes of Shutlingsloe are attractively scattered with heather, and there is more chance of a bright clear day to enjoy those magnificent views during the summer months. The Roaches in Staffordshire, the Wrekin in Shropshire, and the Berwyns and Clwydians of North Wales lift a distant horizon in turn, while nearer to home, Cheshire's highest point, Shining Tor, looks down over the bleak Cat and Fiddle Moors.

The Walk

❶ Leaving the car park, turn left along the road. After passing **Dingers Hollow Farm**, go through a metal gate, following the path along the field edge to reach

The Facts

Terrain Field paths, forest tracks, grassy slopes.

Map OS Explorer OL24 The Peak District.

Starting point Vicarage Quarry free car park (GR SJ 984705).

How to get there & parking From the A54 Congleton–Buxton road, turn where signposted to Wildboarclough, and continue north through that village for one mile. The parking area is on the left. **Sat Nav:** SK11 0BE.

Refreshments On the A537 below Shining Tor, the Peak View Tea Rooms is a very popular licensed establishment with outstanding views. Good-value hearty fare is on offer from 10am to 5pm, Thursday to Sunday throughout the year. ☎ 01298 22103. www.peakviewtearooms.co.uk.

a second gate. Bearing right here, you pass through a third gate to walk along a green track across the hillside. Eventually reaching a kissing gate, you descend to cross a stream on a wooden bridge, then rise again to a kissing gate in a stone wall.

2 Turn left on the lane, climbing quite steeply. At the top, go through a gate on the left, entering the confines of **Macclesfield Forest**, and continue on a broad track signposted to **Shutlingsloe**. After some 400 metres, a lesser path forks off on the left. Take this, keeping right at the next fork in about forty metres, and enjoy views of the Cheshire Plain as you cross the hillside. At length, the path descends to join the broad forest track again.

3 Keep ahead on this track, dipping and then climbing, until just before its highest point, where some wooden steps lead up the bank on your left. Climb the steps; beyond them, a wooden gate admits you to the mountain.

4 Now, simply keep to the paved path, at first climbing gently, and then crossing the moorland plateau to reach a gate in a stone wall. Beyond this, the path swings right, hugging the wall. Stone steps take you over another wall, and a long flight of rough steps leads to the summit. On your left here is a trig point, and beyond it a toposcope set into the rock on the edge.

5 From the south end of the summit, take the obvious path leading into the valley, which is initially steep. After passing through a gate, over a stile and across a wooden bridge, you reach a tarmacked farm track.

summer

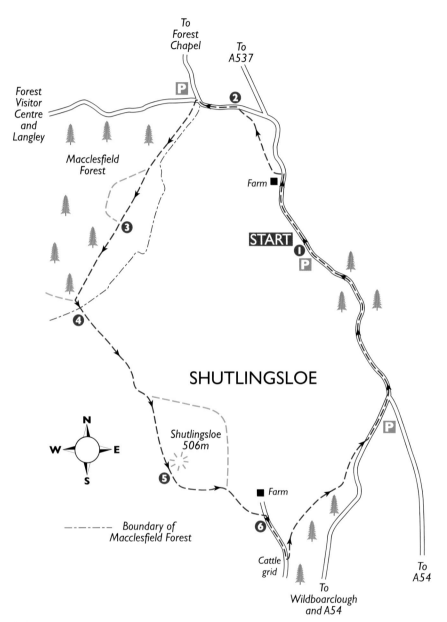

To
Forest
Chapel

To
A537

Forest
Visitor
Centre
and
Langley

P

2

Macclesfield
Forest

Farm ■

START
1
P

3

4

SHUTLINGSLOE

N

W ─ E

S

P

Shutlingsloe
506m

5

■ Farm

6

─ · ─ · ─ Boundary of
Macclesfield Forest

Cattle
grid

To
A54

To
Wildboarclough
and A54

6 Go right on this track, and at the cattle grid, take a track going sharply back to the left. This crosses a stream and passes in front of a house, before continuing above pine woods on the right. After a couple of latched gates, you descend to the road. Turn left, and continue for half a mile to the car park.

Heading across the plateau to Shutlingsloe.

What to look out for –

That view!

Look south to see the long ridge, culminating in the rocky summit of the Roaches, and west to see the Cheshire Plain, with maybe the telescope at Jodrell Bank Observatory glinting in the sunlight. Slightly to the left of this

Trig pillar on Shutlingsloe with Shining Tor behind.

rise the Peckforton Hills, and further back, those of Wales. There's a lot more to be seen, of course, and it's worth consulting that toposcope.

If you have enjoyed this walk

Macclesfield Forest offers many waymarked walks – just pick up a leaflet from the visitor centre. But if it's the hill country that appeals, Cheshire's highest peak, Shining Tor (559 metres), is best climbed starting from Errwood Hall car park, over the border in Derbyshire.

View across the Cheshire Plain from Bulkeley Hill.

11 Burwardsley

5 miles (8 km)

The walk here takes you up Bulkeley Hill, where ancient sweet chestnuts throng the summit. The floor is carpeted with the golden leaves of yesteryear, and if you come sometime in October, this year's prickly-shelled fruit should have fallen among them. It's easy to collect yourself a feast, but just remember that you will be in competition with the squirrels (and other humans!), so you need to get here early in the day for the biggest fruits.

The path across Bulkeley Hill is on Cheshire's Sandstone Trail, and you follow that well-marked route for a couple of miles before branching off into a very different wood. The path through Bodnook Wood is flanked by veteran beech trees, so should the season be right – a little later than the chestnuts – you have a fine display of autumn colour here, too.

Terrain Woodland paths, field paths, lanes.

Map OS Explorer 257 Crewe & Nantwich.

Starting point Free car park off Barracks Lane (GR SJ 522565).

How to get there & parking Burwardsley is just north of the A534, midway between Nantwich and Wrexham. Turn off the A434 where signed, turn right just after the village of Harthill and continue some 2½ miles into the village of Burwardsley. Turn right at the Post Office, uphill, and go right at the junction at the top. The car parking area is on your right. **Sat Nav:** CH3 9PF.

Refreshments The Pheasant Inn, beside the junction a few yards down the road from the car park, offers everything from ham sandwiches to guinea fowl from midday onwards, every day of the week. ☎ 01829 770434 www.thepheasantinn.co.uk.

The Walk

❶ Leaving the car park at the lower end, take the short road opposite, and at the junction, cross directly into **Rock Lane**. Where the road forks, keep right, uphill, and in about 200 metres, you reach a wooden fingerpost beside a kissing gate on the right.

❷ Turn right here; you are now on the **Sandstone Trail**, which you will follow for the next two miles or so. The path runs along the edge of a field, behind a

The Sandstone Trail on Bulkeley Hill.

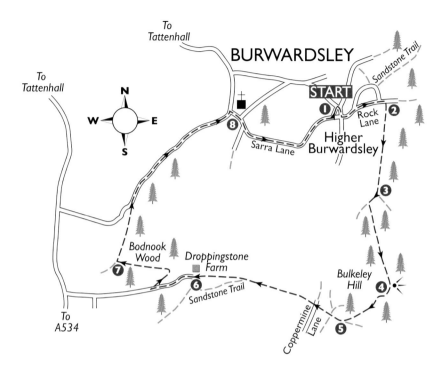

autumn

house, then along more field edges. Reaching a tarmacked lane, bear left to the nearby corner with a signpost.

3 Go right here, along a rough, wide track. After about 150 metres, steps on the left take you into **Bulkeley Hill Wood**. After climbing through oak, silver birch and holly woodland, you meet the first of the sweet chestnuts. The path soon bears right and continues to the summit plateau, where these huge veteran trees thrive in abundance. From here, there is a splendid view east over Crewe, Nantwich and the Cheshire Plain.

4 Follow the Sandstone Trail signs around the rim of the hill to pass through a gap in a fence. Now the path descends, still surrounded by chestnuts, to arrive at a track junction at the edge of the wood.

5 Go right with the Sandstone Trail, crossing a field to reach **Coppermine Lane**. Keep ahead here, on a rough lane with views to the north over the Mersey Estuary. A hundred or so metres after passing a farm, the Sandstone Trail bears left through a kissing gate. Ignore this gate and leave the Sandstone Trail here, instead keeping ahead on a track that is sometimes muddy. After running along the top of a field, the track meets tarmac at the entrance to **Droppingstone Farm**.

6 Keep on the lane now, going downhill and ignoring paths to the right and left. At the woodland edge, look for a gate behind you on the right, marked **Bodnook Cottage**. Turn up the access road (it is a public footpath, though it is not signed as such), and just before the cottage, go over a stile on the left. The path now takes you across the top of a field into **Bodnook Wood**, where beech trees line your buttressed path. The path reaches a high point, then descends to a gated path junction.

7 Turn sharp right, and follow the path diagonally across two fields to emerge on a road. Keep ahead on this for three quarters of a mile to the first road junction, at the edge of **Burwardsley**.

8 Turn right here, and at the church, go right on **Sarra Lane**. In 100 metres or so, where the lane splits, bear left downhill to cross the stream. The narrow lane now climbs almost continuously, until after half a mile you reach the junction at the top of the hill. Turn left to return to the car park.

What to look out for –

Rare woodland

Bulkeley Hill stands at the southern end of the Peckfortons, Cheshire's long sandstone ridge, which extends from Frodsham south into Shropshire. These hills are covered in ancient broadleaf woodland that is now rare elsewhere in the county. Enjoy the variety of beautiful trees on this walk.

Sweet chestnut trees on Bulkeley Hill.

If you have enjoyed this walk

Burwardsley is a good central location for exploring the Sandstone Trail. You could continue heading south from Point 6, going over Raw Head, the highest point of the trail at 227 metres. Or you could walk north from the start, going past Peckforton Castle to Beeston Castle. Download a leaflet of the Sandstone Trail that includes a couple of circular walks at www.sandstoneridge.org.uk/doc/D225692.pdf.

Waiting at Marbury Lock.

12 Marbury

4 miles (6.4 km)

Red berries on the hawthorn, dark purple on the elder, bright orange hips on the dog rose, and scarlet clusters on the rowan: in autumn, the woods and hedgerows yield their colourful bounty, and on this off-the-beaten-track walk you should see it in profusion.

Pushed against Cheshire's southern border, Marbury is only a few miles from Whitchurch, but nowhere could feel further from urbanisation than its fields, woods, low-lying meres and scattered farms. The village is a rural idyll in itself: half-timbered cottages clustered round an ancient church of red sandstone and overlooking the tranquil waters of a mere. Few ramblers cross the fields here, and the lanes are strangers to traffic, but on this walk, your wake-up call comes at the end, in the form of the Llangollen Canal. This is Britain's most popular leisure waterway, and it is likely to be busy even this late in the season. You may well meet boats queuing to go through the lock as you return to Marbury.

The Facts

autumn

Terrain Cross-field paths, where the grass may be long underfoot; quiet lanes; canal towpath.

Map OS Explorer 257 Crewe & Nantwich.

Starting point The triangular green with the oak tree in the centre of Marbury (GR SJ 561457).

How to get there & parking Marbury is just north of Whitchurch. From the A534–A49 junction at Ridley, continue south on the A49 for about four miles to turn left where signposted to Marbury. Keep left at the first junction (unsigned), then follow signs for a further two miles to reach the village centre. At The Swan for patrons, otherwise on roadsides in the village, or in the large lay-by on the road to Norbury. **Sat Nav:** SY13 4LS.

Refreshments You won't miss The Swan Inn at the heart of Marbury. A large establishment with ample outdoor seating, it is very happy to welcome walkers, and suggests a walk or two of its own. With a menu that could perhaps be described as up-market, food is served from midday onwards, every day ☎ 01948 522860 www.swanatmarbury.co.uk.

The Walk

1 From the green, with its oak tree – planted to commemorate the Battle of Waterloo in 1815 – walk downhill on **Hollins Lane** in the direction of **Whitchurch**. About 200 metres after the last house, take a path on the right, heading across the field towards **Big Mere**. Approaching the mere, a wooden gate on the left admits you to a waterside path. Follow this through two more gates to emerge on a field that can be boggy after wet weather. The meres in this area were formed where retreating glaciers left pockets of ice behind, at the end of the Ice Age. No stream flows in or out of the meres; they each have a bed of clay, and maintain their level by natural seepage from the surrounding countryside.

2 Now keep the woodland on your left to pass between two telegraph poles, then go right to reach a large oak tree in a hollow. From this tree, wind up the shallow valley to arrive at a stile beneath hawthorns in the top corner of the field. Beyond this, the path continues up the left-hand edge of the field to reach a pair of stiles beside holly trees in the far corner. In the next field, bear diagonally right, uphill, to the top right-hand corner.

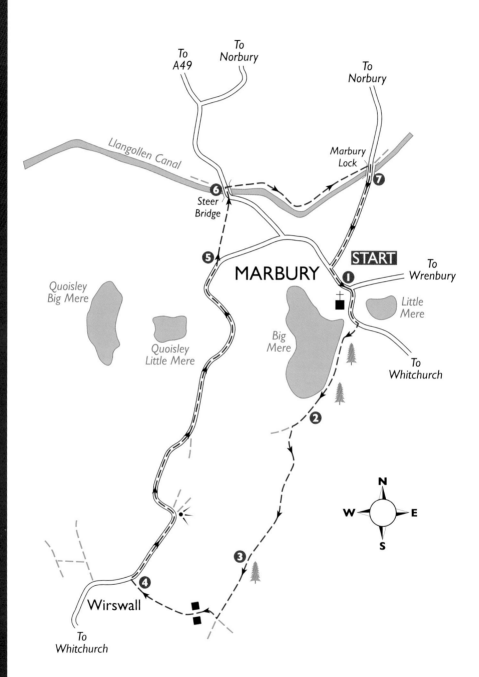

To
A49

To
Norbury

To
Norbury

Llangollen Canal

Marbury
Lock

6

Steer
Bridge

7

5

START

MARBURY

To
Wrenbury

1

Little
Mere

Quoisley
Big Mere

Quoisley
Little Mere

Big
Mere

To
Whitchurch

2

N
W · E
S

3

4

Wirswall

To
Whitchurch

3 Here, a stile leads to another field. Bear left, keeping a tree-lined hollow on your left, and maintain this direction to cross the field to another stile in a fence, well left of a barn. Keep ahead across this narrow field to reach a stile with a wooden signpost alongside. Do not cross this stile; instead, turn right along the fence in the direction of **Wirswall**. After a stile, you continue between farm buildings and then walk up the farm access track to arrive at a tarmacked lane.

4 Turn right on this narrow lane, which in autumn is scattered with acorns from the many oak trees alongside. At a corner, there is a picnic table, from which a short detour into the field opposite offers a fine view back across the fields to **Marbury**. Ahead here are the two **Quoisley Meres**, with the **Peckforton Hills** rising behind. Continue down this lane, which soon descends. After something over a mile you pass a large farm on the left, and after a further 300 metres or so, you meet a signpost marked '**Canal**' pointing over the fields on the left.

5 Follow the direction of the signpost to reach a stile immediately left of shrubby **Hadley Covert**, in the middle of the field. A fenced track now takes you alongside the covert, after which another stile gives access to a field. Cross this directly to reach a tarmacked road, and turn left to cross the canal bridge.

View from Wirswall Hill over Marbury.

6 Immediately after the bridge, turn left down the steps to gain the towpath and then left again to pass beneath the bridge. There follows a lovely stretch under drooping conifers. After half a mile, you reach **Marbury Lock**.

7 Leave the canal here to turn right up **School Lane**. A few minutes' more walking, and you are back in Marbury. At the T-junction, turn left to return to the green at the centre of the village. Just before reaching the green, don't miss a visit to **Marbury Church**, up a short lane on the right.

What to look out for –

Marbury Church

If you come in October, the hedges in these fields and lanes will be laden with fruits and berries of all kinds. If you have children with you, they might like to count how many different ones they can find. Ten would be very good; fifteen would deserve a prize! In Marbury itself, meanwhile, don't go home without a peep at the church. Dedicated to St Michael and All Angels, it dates from the 15th

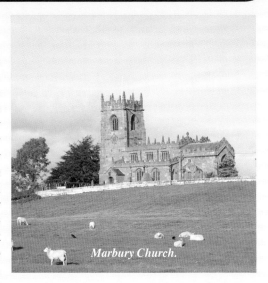

Marbury Church.

century. Look out for the curious gargoyles, and the handsome sundial that was added to commemorate the millennium. Can you see that the tower is leaning? No? Well, it's only a little off true.

If you have enjoyed this walk

You might like to walk further along the Llangollen Canal. Heading south from Marbury towards Whitchurch, you would pass the fascinating Grindley Brook staircase locks, while to the north, the village of Wrenbury with its two pubs is just a two-mile stroll away – it's longer by road!

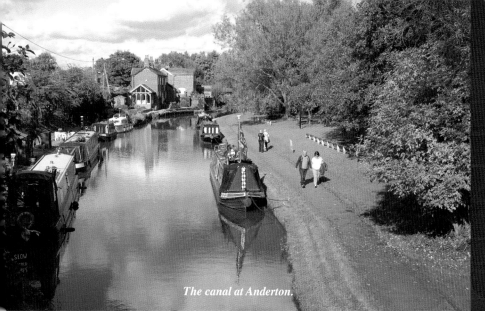

The canal at Anderton.

13 Anderton

3½ miles (5.6 km)

The nature park at Anderton is one of nine countryside sites that come together under the title of Northwich Woodlands. Truly, this site is a miracle of reclamation: salt extraction and the chemical industry took a heavy toll here over many years. Today, pools fill the old mining sites, rare plants and woods of silver birch thrive on the residues of soda ash, and the Trent and Mersey Canal running through its heart carries pleasure craft, rather than commercial barges. The whole area is criss-crossed with paths, and it all makes for some easy, pleasant walking.

The walk here takes in Anderton Nature Park and, to the north, Marbury Country Park. Both have fine birch woods, in which, come autumn, fungi flourish. This isn't a long walk, because you will want to get off the path and hunt around a bit, and that takes time. The fungi are there in plenty, but for anyone who really wants to get serious, fungal forays are staged here every year in mid-September. Apparently there are more than seventy species to be found!

Fungi or not, this is a pleasant short walk in its own right, and you are sure to want to see more of Northwich Woodlands. Before you leave, though, you must visit the Anderton Boat Lift, just around the corner from the Nature Park. Constructed in 1875 to carry boats between the canal and the River Weaver, it strides the fifty-foot drop between the two like some monster from science fiction. Restored and in full working order, you could take a ride on it while you are here, or simply sit in the café and watch the action.

61

Terrain Gravel paths and earth tracks.

Map OS Explorer 267 Northwich & Delamere Forest.

Starting point Anderton Boat Lift Visitor Centre car park (GR SJ 650753).

How to get there & parking From the A533 Northwich–Runcorn road, turn right immediately after crossing the bridge over the Weaver before Barnton. The Anderton Boat Lift Visitor Centre is also signed from the A559 Northwich–Warrington road, about two miles from Anderton. Park in the pay and display car park. **Sat Nav:** CW9 6FW.

Refreshments The coffee shop at Anderton Boat Lift serves light lunches, along with hot drinks and home-made cake.

The Walk

❶ Leave the car park on the main tarmacked track between the dragonfly gates, and keep right to descend to the riverside. At the bottom of the hill on your left is a pond too salty for frogs or fish, allowing dragonfly larvae to thrive unchecked. At the riverside, the factory on the far bank is the **Winnington chemical works**, now closed after a hundred and forty years of soda ash production. You could divert to the right, here, and walk along the riverbank to get a good view of the

The Anderton Boat Lift.

autumn

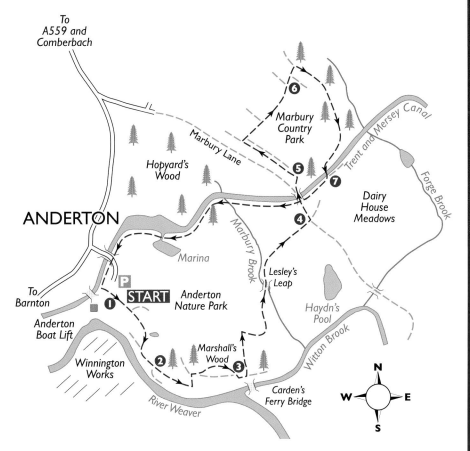

boat lift. Follow the path as it bends away from the river and reaches a signed path junction.

2 Keep left here, going up a long flight of steps to enter **Marshall's Wood**, an area of silver birch woodland which is distinctive for the reason that it grows on raw lime waste; in other areas, such waste has been covered with clay before native trees were planted. To see the best of the wood, go left at the first junction; then, at the T-junction, go right on the wide track, and then left at the following junction.

3 Reaching a multiple junction, turn left. A few metres further on, just after the bridge, take the first path on your left, which soon emerges into meadowland. Arriving at a signposted T-junction, turn right, and continue on this wide track, which crosses **Marbury Brook** at an attractive spot known as **Lesley's Leap**. Keeping ahead, you reach the tarmacked **Marbury Lane**.

CHESHIRE *Year Round Walks*

4 Turn left on the lane. Immediately after crossing the canal bridge, take a track leading into woods on the right. Now you are in **Marbury Country Park**; the winding track you are on soon reaches a signpost.

5 Turn left here, on a track still within the woods but with glimpses of a field through the trees on your right. Where the track meets tarmac, turn right to pass between fields, and ignore tracks crossing them on your left.

6 Where the tarmac bends sharply right, keep ahead on a rough track through the trees. Soon reaching a T-junction, turn right on a lovely wide track through the woods. At length, this track reaches the canal-side and a wrought-iron footbridge.

7 Cross the canal on this bridge; then, keeping the canal on your right, continue on the towpath all the way back to **Anderton**. Eventually, the boat lift is directly ahead of you, and a road on the left leads up to the car park.

What to look out for –

The fungi, of course!

If you get really lucky, you might spot the showiest of them all, the red-with-white-spots fly agaric. If not, you can always join one of the fungal forays that take place at both Anderton Nature Park and Marbury Country Park, as well as at many other sites in Cheshire, including National Trust properties.

If you have enjoyed this walk

You will surely want to see more of Northwich Woodlands. Download a map at http://foam.merseyforest.org.uk/wp-content/uploads/2018/07/Northwich-Woodlands-Map.pdf and return another day.

Little Moreton Hall.

14 Little Moreton Hall

5 miles (8 km)

Autumn is traditionally a season of superstition and ghostly happenings, particularly around Halloween and the subsequent All Saints' and All Souls' Days. The days are getting shorter, the evenings more gloomy, and it all helps the imagination along. Well, you can't really expect to see a ghost on this walk, but a visit to Little Moreton Hall beforehand could give you a reasonable chance. In this remarkable half-timbered Tudor mansion, a 'grey lady' has been known to brush silently past visitors in the Long Gallery, and other spectres have apparently been seen in the house and in the road nearby as well.

The Tudors were extremely superstitious and used all manner of talismans to ward off such visitations, but no doubt the night-time creaking of the timbers in this wonderfully eccentric building fed their fears. Little Moreton Hall is now in the care of the National Trust, and every autumn they pay homage to its otherworldly connections with a few related events of their own.

Having taken leave of the phantoms, it's time to have a bite to eat in the excellent National Trust tea rooms and blow away any remaining spooky cobwebs on this walk. It's a simple circuit through the fields and lanes south of the mansion, and it takes in an old mill, an 18th-century country house and a stretch of the Macclesfield Canal. Oh, and you'll be walking 'widdershins' – but surely no one believes in bad luck nowadays?

Terrain Field paths, some with long grass in autumn; country lanes; canal towpath.

Map OS Explorer 268 Wilmslow, Macclesfield & Congleton.

Starting point National Trust Little Moreton Hall (GR SJ 831588).

How to get there & parking Little Moreton Hall is signed off the A34 Congleton–Kidsgrove road, about midway between those two towns. Park in the free car park. **Sat Nav:** CW12 4SD.

Refreshments Snacks, light lunches and cream teas are on offer in Little Moreton Hall's tea rooms. Note that they are only accessed through the house itself. The Rising Sun at Scholar Green has an extensive menu; food is served at lunchtimes and in the evenings during the week, and all day at weekends. ☎ 01782 776235. www.risingsunscholargreen.co.uk.

The Walk _____

1 Leaving the access road to Little Moreton Hall, turn right alongside the A34 (there is a narrow pavement on the opposite side), and in 200 metres, turn left up the drive to **Cuttleford Farm**. Where the drive bends left, keep straight ahead to find a stile taking you behind the house and greenhouses into a field. Keep the hedge on your left, and just before the next field entrance, take a signed path skirting the field on the left. This soon bends right alongside the hedge and continues to meet a lane.

Approaching Bridge 86 on the Macclesfield Canal.

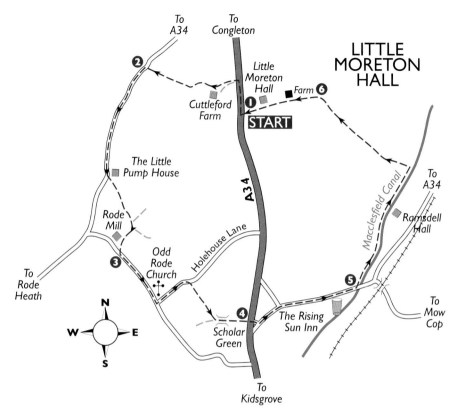

2 Turn left, and keep to this lane for about half a mile. It is signed as part of the **South Cheshire Way**, but it is fairly busy even so – take care! After passing **Higher Smallwood Farm**, turn left into the driveway of a property named **The Little Pump House**, and immediately turn right to join a footpath, soon entering a field with a stream. Cross the stream on a plank bridge, and continue to a stile in the far left corner. In the next big field (which can be boggy), keep the hedge on your left to reach a stile onto a farm access road. Go right, and pass a dilapidated former mill before reaching a road.

3 Turn left onto the roadside pavement, and continue for 400 metres to the curiously named **Odd Rode Church**. The churchyard is full of ancient yew trees, bearing red, waxy berries in autumn. Turn left here into **Holehouse Lane**. At the bottom of the hill, immediately before a bridge, go over a stile on the right to enter a field. Walk uphill on a track; then, ignoring gates to the left and right, continue across a field with a wire fence on your right. At the far corner, a stile leads to a hedged path. Turn left, pass some houses, and continue to the A34 in **Scholar Green**.

autumn

4 Cross the A34 to the road opposite, and turn left. The road bends right and climbs gently. After half a mile skirting a residential area, and just after the **Rising Sun Inn**, you arrive at a canal bridge. Turn left immediately before it onto **Moorson Avenue**, then find a stile on the right to access the canal towpath.

5 Keep the canal on your right, and continue for half a mile, passing the handsome 18th-century **Ramsdell Hall** on the opposite bank. This house, too, is said to have a resident ghost: the daughter of a previous owner, accidentally killed in a duel between competing swains. At the next bridge, numbered 86, two kissing gates lead you away from the canal to a rough track. Turn left on this track, and continue to the stile at its end, bending right alongside the hedge in the following field. Keep the hedge on your right in the next field also, following a clear, pleasant track.

6 In the third field, bear diagonally left towards the farm buildings on the opposite side. Kissing gates at the top left-hand corner take you into a final field. Keep ahead beside the hedge to reach another gate onto the farm access road. Continue ahead to return to Little Moreton Hall.

What to look out for –

The Knot Garden

Little Moreton Hall itself, which is over five hundred years old, is a strange, top-heavy, ornately half-timbered building, with crooked walls and rolling floors adding to its appeal. Don't miss the knot garden at the rear, and

The Knot Garden at Little Moreton Hall.

come earlier in the autumn to enjoy such rarities as quince and medlar in the orchard garden. Entry is free for National Trust members; there's a fee for all others.

If you have enjoyed this walk

The hill of Mow Cop, with its ruined summit folly, has been sitting tantalisingly on the horizon throughout this walk. Mow Cop is actually the last in a thirty-five-mile line of gritstone peaks that stretches north from here to Disley. To walk it all, download the Gritstone Trail leaflet from www.cheshireeast.gov.uk.

Beech trees on Artists Lane.

15 Alderley Edge

4½ miles (7.2 km)

Everyone enjoys a good walk in the woods in autumn, and where could be better for taking in those rich, coppery colours than Alderley Edge? Across this abrupt, red sandstone escarpment spread woods of oak, pine, holly, and that king of all autumn trees, the beech. The National Trust has care of these woods now, and this walk takes you to the farthest corner, where a 'cathedral' of beeches, huge trees planted more than two hundred years ago, stands on the slopes of a steep valley. In autumn, their leaves shade from yellow to deepest bronze, and the floor is carpeted with the still-golden leaves of previous years.

Those 'cathedral' beeches are by no means the only ones on this route. At the beginning of the walk, the beeches flanking Artists Lane are equally impressive – and as you walk down that lane, it's fascinating to remember that in one of those tree-clad banks, a gold ingot was found some twenty-five years ago. Maybe you won't come across an ingot on this walk, but similar discoveries have been made elsewhere on Alderley Edge, including caches of jewellery and Roman coins. Other treasures hidden from your gaze are the ancient mine shafts in the slopes, with rich seams of copper and lead. And then there are the legends of the Edge: stories of the wizard, knights and white horses that haunt the caves, and which inspired Alan Garner to write his children's classic *The Weirdstone of Brisingamen*. Enjoy your walk, then maybe read the book!

CHESHIRE Year Round Walks

Terrain Forest paths, firm-surfaced tracks, quiet lane.

Map OS Explorer 268 Wilmslow, Macclesfield & Congleton.

Starting point National Trust Alderley Edge car park (GR SJ 859772).

How to get there & parking In the town of Alderley Edge, follow signs for the B5087 to Macclesfield. The car park is on the left in one mile; a fee is payable; free for National Trust members. **Sat Nav:** SK10 4UB.

Refreshments The Wizard Tearoom, adjacent to the car park, is perfect for an all-day breakfast, a light lunch, or just tea and home-made cake, and is open every day.

The Walk

1 From the car park, walk through to the **Wizard Tearoom** and the **Wizard Inn**. Here, cross the road directly into **Artists Lane**, and continue downhill between the banks of splendid beeches.

2 At the bottom of the hill, take a bridleway signed off the road on the right. After going through a wooden gate, continue uphill to the right on a broad track, and at the cross-tracks, continue ahead. Reaching the top of the slope, the track bears left to a gate into a field. Do not go through the gate; instead, turn right in front of it, before reaching the edge of the woodland. This path soon becomes a lovely hedged track between fields, and continues to the road.

3 Cross the road, and keep directly ahead on a track between fields, soon reaching a fine viewpoint at **Castle Rock**. Apparently, an Earl of Chester decided to build a castle here around nine hundred years ago, but didn't get any further than the foundations. The view you have is to the north, across Manchester, with the Peak District over to the right. Turn right, and continue on the firm path along the edge of the cliff. Eventually, you have a stone wall on your right, and you can see a mound topped with a block of stone ahead. The stone commemorates the beacon that was lit on this site to warn of the approaching Spanish Armada in 1588. There were no trees on the hill at the time!

4 From the beacon, take the track straight ahead of you, and at the first cross-tracks, turn left. Continue on this path, ignoring all side turnings, until you arrive at a T-junction, with the **Edge** ahead of you once more. On the way, you

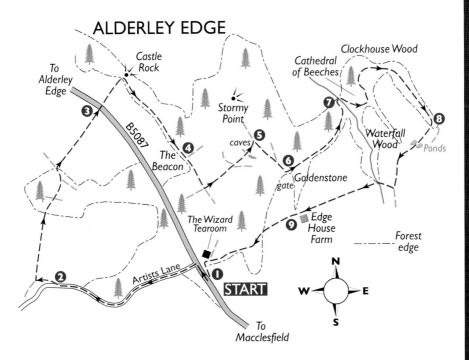

ALDERLEY EDGE

will pass through a sort of ditch with rocky sides. Quarry workers once lived in caves here.

5 To the left at this junction is **Stormy Point**, another rocky viewpoint, but you go to the right, continuing past a track leading back down the slope to reach a wooden gate. Just beyond the gate, you can see a huge stone on the left. This is the **Goldenstone**, a rock of conglomerate, alien to these parts. It is thought it may have been carried here in the Bronze Age.

6 Do not go through the wooden gate, but instead turn left down the slope. Now you are heading into **Waterfall Wood**, named for the cascade in the stream at its heart. Keep ahead, walking downhill on the main path, to reach a T-junction. Turn left here, still going downhill and now with the stream in the deep cleft on your right. At the bottom, with a field ahead, the path bears right to cross the narrow stream on two stepping stones.

7 Now the obvious path climbs, with those splendid 'cathedral' beeches soon appearing on either side. At the top of the hill, bear left with the path, then right very soon afterwards, and continue on the broad track through **Clockhouse Wood**, on the side of the slope. At the lowest point, above **Clockhouse Farm**,

Looking back over the ponds in Point 8.

a buttressed balcony path takes you over a muddy patch, after which you continue to the top of the hill.

8 Here, go over a stile beside a gate on the right, and continue in the field with a hedge on your right. The path soon takes you between ponds, afterwards reaching a path junction. Turn right on a descending fenced path between fields. Ignore a path on the right, then climb, crossing two stiles to reach **Edge House Farm** at the top of the hill.

9 Cross the wide drive to a narrow track opposite, running between fields again. Where this emerges on a wide track in the woods, turn left, and keep ahead through a wooden gate to reach the car park.

What to look out for –

Caves

There are so many curious historical and legendary sites to be found on Alderley Edge. Pick up the leaflet *What Lies Beneath* from the Wizard Tearoom, and explore some more.

Quarry workers' caves in Point 4.

If you have enjoyed this walk

Not far from Alderley Edge is another National Trust property, Quarry Bank Mill. If you take the path to the north of the mill alongside the River Bollin, you will again encounter some really magnificent beeches. Visit the National Trust website (www.nationaltrust.org.uk) for more details.

autumn

Looking out over the marshes at Parkgate.

16 Parkgate

3 miles (4.8 km)

Walking along the promenade beside the marshes at Parkgate, could you ever think that this was once a major passenger port with frequent crossings to Ireland? Well, it was, and the town proudly boasts that Handel sailed from Parkgate on his way to Dublin for the first performance of *Messiah* in 1742. The scene has changed a lot since then! The Dee Estuary has silted up, a process helped by the planting of cordgrass, and Parkgate now fronts a wide expanse of salt marsh, much appreciated by migrating birds and various wildfowl. The whole area is an RSPB reserve, so don't forget your binoculars.

Not too long and not too muddy, this is a perfect walk for a winter's day. You are pretty sure to spot some of the reserve's winter visitors, and from the higher land behind Parkgate you can relish the splendid view across the estuary, where Welsh hills lift the horizon. For the end of the ramble, the handsome half-timbered buildings of Parkgate are home to a surprisingly wide range of pubs and cafés. Or maybe you can face down the winter cold, and go instead for the home-made ice cream for which this little town is famous!

The Facts

Terrain Firm paths, mostly dry field paths, roads and lanes. An almost flat walk with no stiles.

Map OS Explorer 266 Wirral & Chester.

Starting point Old Baths car park (GR SJ 273790).

How to get there & parking Parkgate is signed from the A540 Chester–West Kirby road. Travel north on the seafront road to reach the Boathouse Inn at a sharp bend. Here, go straight ahead under the height barrier, and continue for 250 metres to the car park. **Sat Nav:** CH64 6RL.

Refreshments The Boat House, near the car park, has a comprehensive menu and a particularly fine view over the marshes, ☎ 0151 336 4187, www.theboathouseparkgate.co.uk. More eateries can be found along the seafront, where you can also sample Parkgate's very own ice cream.

The Walk

1 Leave the car park by the path at its north end, which almost immediately swings left to run along the sea wall. Continue along this raised path, which has views over the salt marsh, and after about 500 metres, ignore the path on the right crossing the golf course (although it could represent a shortcut). After a narrow section of path beside a high beech hedge, some steps lead down to **Cottage Lane**.

2 Turn right up Cottage Lane. After about 400 metres, you cross over the **Wirral Way**, a twelve-mile walking and cycling route along the trackbed of a former railway. Keep ahead to the road junction at the top of the hill.

3 Here, turn right into the cobbled **Gayton Farm Road**, at its end bearing right on a descending earthen track. Shortly, pass the old **Gayton Well** in the bank on the left, and continue with the golf course on your right.

4 Ignore the path crossing the golf course (this is the other end of the path you saw at Point 1), and keep ahead, winding through the trees. Soon, the path enters the golf course itself, hugging the left-hand edge to reach a signed kissing gate.

5 Through the gate, maintain your direction over a field to cross a small brook and arrive at another gate. After heavy rain, there could be some water

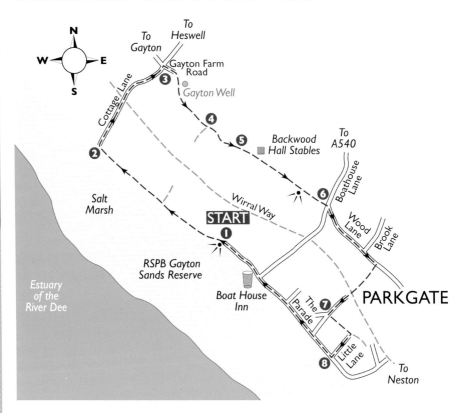

flowing in the channel in the middle of this field, but it should be easy to step over it. Passing through the gate, you now have **Backwood Hall Stables** on your left. Keep straight ahead along the clearly signed route, which becomes a wide earthen track. There are fine views across the estuary to the Clwydian Hills at this point.

6 Reaching the gate at the end of the track, cross **Boathouse Lane** with care, and carry on along **Wood Lane** opposite. About 100 metres after passing the end of **Brook Lane**, take a track on the right, alongside a fence. This soon passes under an old railway bridge, now carrying the **Wirral Way**. Pass the school, and continue for about 200 metres to a road junction.

7 Turn left here into a narrow, hedged path signposted to some of the houses in **Mostyn Gardens**. This path is known as the **Ropewalk**, and is absolutely straight, as it was once used by ropemakers to lay out their ropes. After passing the children's playground, turn right into **Little Lane**, which descends to the seafront.

winter

Seafront at Parkgate.

8 Take a few moments to investigate the toposcope and information panels in the viewpoint opposite, then simply walk along the seafront, with the marsh on your left, to return to the car park.

What to look out for –

Birds in the salt marshes

Birds seen in the salt marshes at this time of year include curlews, egrets and pink-footed geese. In the skies above, and particularly at high tide, birds of prey like hen harriers, merlins and short-eared owls can be seen seeking out small rodents, driven from hiding by the incoming water. Late winter is renowned for its especially high tides, so look up the tide table for Liverpool (www.ntslf.org/tides/tidepred), note

that Parkgate is approximately twenty minutes later, and maybe time your walk accordingly.

If you have enjoyed this walk

There are plenty more bird reserves in Cheshire. Burton Mere Wetlands, just a few miles south of Parkgate, offers walks, hides and a visitor centre.

Woods in the snow.

17 Delamere

4½ miles (7.2 km)

Woods in the snow are magic! Falling snow wraps everything in silence; the grey tones of winter change to black and white; what colour there is seems brighter – the shiny green of the holly and its scarlet berries, the orange breast of the robin. And then there are the tracks on the ground, evidence of all that forest wildlife you can't see at any other time. So if it snows – and we don't see it that often, these days – get over to Delamere Forest and take this walk.

Being on a well-used B-road, Delamere should be fairly accessible in light snow, and the route here starts right beside that road at Hatchmere. The path through Hatchmere Nature Reserve is of the less-trodden kind, winding through thickets of vegetation and picking its way between ponds. Beyond this, you are on the well-surfaced tracks of the main forest, skirting wide Blakemere Moss, before heading off through a quiet corner of the woods again for the return.

Snow will slow down your progress, so should this route prove too far, several shortcuts have been detailed. But why wait for that unpredictable white stuff? This is an excellent walk at any time of year, and if you come in summer, you can bring your swimming costume: Hatchmere is a very popular spot for wild swimming!

Terrain Wide, firm-surfaced tracks in the forest. The path around Hatchmere can be muddy in places, so stout footwear is recommended.

Map OS Explorer 267 Northwich & Delamere Forest.

Starting point Roadside lay-by on the B5152 at Hatchmere, just north of the Carriers Inn pub (GR SJ 554721).

How to get there & parking Hatchmere is on the B5152, four miles south of Frodsham. Coming from Frodsham, the lay-by is on the right immediately before the Carriers Inn, with the picnic area opposite. Alternatively, the picnic area across the road has pay and display parking, but this is sometimes closed. **Sat Nav: WA6 6NL.**

Refreshments The Carriers Inn has a wide menu, including some most exotic burgers, and serves food every day except Monday from noon onwards. The visitor centre in Delamere Forest also has a café – turn right at Post 16. ☎ 01928 787877. www.carriersinnhatchmerelake.com.

The Walk

❶ From the lay-by, cross the road to walk on the pavement, heading away from the **Carriers Inn**. Just before the road bends left, take a path on the left running around the edge of the lake. The path weaves in and out between the marshy areas of **Hatchmere**. With its dense vegetation and swamps, Hatchmere can sometimes feel like a miniature version of the Everglades. But whereas the Everglades is effectively a river, Hatchmere is a kettle hole, the result of a pocket of ice left by retreating glaciers some ten thousand years ago. After maybe half a mile on this narrow track, beside an information panel, yellow arrows direct you to take a few paces to the right and then go left again. Soon afterwards, the path emerges onto a wide, hard-surfaced track.

❷ Turn left here, and continue for about 250 metres to the road. (A left turn here will quickly return you to the crossroads in Hatchmere, with the Carriers on your left.) To continue with the main walk, turn right, and continue along the road for about 300 metres to where wide tracks branch off left and right. Turn right on the wide track signed as **Delamere Loop**. Now you have numbered posts to help you: keep ahead at Post 28, go left at Post 29, and turn left again at Post 30, winding attractively around more kettle holes. Eventually you meet signs for the **Sandstone Trail**, and arrive at the road.

winter

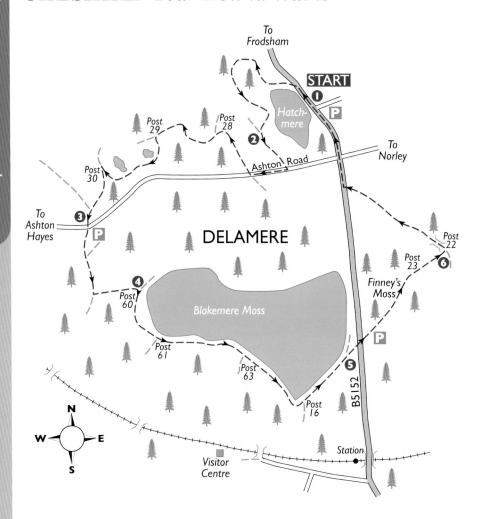

③ Again, a left turn would get you quickly back to base, but to continue, cross the road, following the Sandstone Trail signs up the path to the right of the car park. Now take the second track on the left, signed with the red arrow of the **Delamere Way**, which soon brings you down to the edge of **Blakemere Moss** at Post 60. *Moss* is the local term for a peat bog, formed when dead vegetation accumulating in the bed of a mere finally fills it, rising above the water.

④ Turn right here, and keep ahead round Blakemere Moss, passing Posts 61, 63 and 16. Soon after the latter, bear right to meet the B5152.

winter

A robin looking out over the trees.

5 Again, turning left on the road here would take you back to the Carriers. To carry on, cross the road into the entrance to **Whitefield car park**. About forty metres in, take a track dipping down on the left, which soon runs along the edge of **Finney's Moss**. After about half a mile, pass Post 23 beside the path, and continue to Post 22.

6 Turn left here. Where the path swings right, keep ahead across a waymarked wooden bridge, then bend right through the trees to eventually climb a bank. The path continues alongside a hedge, then passes between houses to emerge on the main road. Turn right here, and keep ahead at the crossroads to return to the **Carriers Inn**.

winter

What to look out for –

Animal prints in the snow

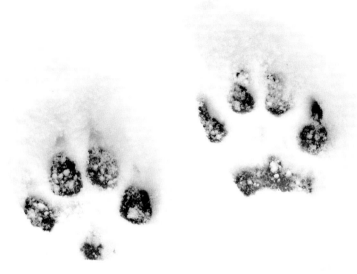

Rabbits and squirrels bound, with four feet together, but squirrel toes and maybe claws can be seen. And those paw prints just could be a fox – or a dog, of course. In summer, butterflies enjoy these dappled glades, and you can look out for some of the rare dragonflies and damselflies on the meres. Birds like woodpeckers and treecreepers are all-year-rounders. There's always plenty to see!

If you have enjoyed this walk

There are more woods to explore in the snow at Northwich (see Walk 13) and at Macclesfield (see Walk 5). If mosses and meres particularly interest you, head south to the Ellesmere area and Whixall Moss.

On the Whitegate Way.

18 Whitegate Way

4 miles (6.4 km)

Y ou can almost hear the heavy goods trains puffing as you walk along the Whitegate Way. The railway here was opened in the 1870s to carry rock salt from the mines at Winsford to join the main Chester–Manchester line at Cuddington. Almost a century later, the last train made that journey, and the Whitegate Way is now one of Cheshire's many restored trackbeds. Its firm, earthen surface means you can still enjoy a mud-free rural walk when the footpaths around are at their winter-wettest.

The countryside here is quintessential Cheshire: fields, farms, woods and ponds, all of which can be appreciated from the embankments and cuttings of the six-mile-long track. It would not be too difficult to walk the whole length and back in a day, but this short route starts from the midpoint at Whitegate Station, and after heading up the line, branches off to visit the ponds of Newchurch Common. These are a birdwatcher's paradise at any time of year, but winter is surely the best time for the wildfowl. Maybe take your binoculars and bird book.

At the end of the day, there's a treat waiting in the station building: now housing a café, it serves the most delicious home-made cakes!

Terrain Hard, earthen track and easy, well-defined paths. Can be muddy in places. An almost flat walk.

Map OS Explorer 267 Northwich & Delamere Forest.

Starting point Whitegate Station (GR SJ 615680).

How to get there & parking Whitegate Station is about two miles west of Winsford. It is signed off the A54, a mile and a half east of its crossing with the A49, and also from the A556 at Sandiway. There is free parking and toilets at the station. **Sat Nav:** CW7 2QE.

Refreshments The homely little station café offers tea and cakes, soup, sandwiches and the like, and has both indoor and outdoor seating. There are also picnic tables at the station. In the village of Whitegate (1½ miles north), the attractive Plough Inn offers a wide selection of food throughout the day. ☎ 01606 889455. www.ploughwhitegate.com.

The Walk _____

❶ Leaving the station, walk under the road bridge and up the track. After about fifteen minutes' walking, you pass the entrance to **Newchurch Common**

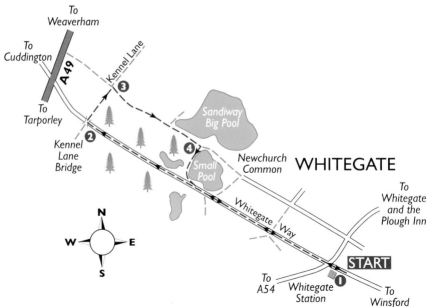

84

Kennel Lane Bridge on the Whitegate Way.

on your right. You might want to divert for a quick look at **Sandiway Small Pool** and its wildlife here – although you will see more of this pond later on. Soon after the Newchurch Common entrance, a bench overlooks an attractive small pond surrounded by woodland, and after a further half mile or so, you arrive at the old, brick-built **Kennel Lane Bridge**.

2 Walk up the ramp, and turn right to cross the bridge. You are now in **Kennel Lane**, with an activity centre behind the fencing on your right. In about 300 metres, you reach a barrier and a track junction.

3 Turn right here to follow the byway. There may well be some mud here after wet weather, but this is much reduced after you pass the farm at the top of the hill. Continuing beyond the farm, you can see the first lake, known as **Sandiway Big Pool**, behind trees on your left. After about 400 metres, it is possible to get down to the shore of this lake, while on the right, a gap in the bank beside a redundant stile gives access to another lake, **Sandiway Small Pool**. Both these lakes are the result of sand quarrying.

winter

4 Turn right through the gap in the bank mentioned above, and take the broad track ahead around Sandiway Small Pool. A lesser track, used by fishermen, runs along the shore below you. The broad track eventually bears left around the end of the lake, and soon afterwards, a fence appears ahead. A gap in this allows you back on to the **Whitegate Way**. Turn left, and simply retrace your steps to the station.

What to look out for –

The ponds of Newchurch Common

Little evidence of the railway remains, with the exception of the load gauge at Whitegate Station. But just walking along the track, with the trees arching overhead, gives a real sense of the past.

Sandiway Small Pool.

The ponds of Newchurch Common well merit extra investigation. You are pretty certain to see moorhens, grebes and Canada geese, and maybe teal and wigeon, but how about a red-crested pochard or a smew? Both of these rarities have been seen here in recent times.

If you have enjoyed this walk

There are plenty more disused railway lines that have been converted for public use in Cheshire. Not too far away, you could try the short Salt Line at Alsager (see Walk 4) or the adjacent Wheelock Rail Trail. Over in the west, there's the Wirral Way, twelve miles of hard-surfaced track, while in the north, the Trans Pennine Trail makes good use of the route of the one-time Warrington and Stockport Railway (see Walk 19). Then, near Congleton, you have the pretty Biddulph Valley Way, and further north at Macclesfield, the splendid ten-mile-long Middlewood Way paralleling the Macclesfield Canal. There's really no need to get muddy feet in Cheshire!

The moat at Dunham Massey.

19 *Dunham Massey*

7½ or 6 miles (12 or 9.6 km)

Chaste snowdrop, venturous harbinger of spring,
And pensive monitor of fleeting years.

Wordsworth's eulogy on a snowdrop certainly isn't as well-known as that on a certain other flower, but it's surprising he was able to write about them at all: they were few and far between in Britain in 1819. Most of the many species now around hail originally from the Continent; some were actually brought back by soldiers returning from the Crimean War. It matters not a bit. We all love their delicate faces, braving the very coldest weeks of the year.

Snowdrops in the wild are not that easy to come by, but if you want to be sure of a real spectacle, take this walk through the grounds of National Trust-owned Dunham Massey, where some three hundred thousand create a magical carpet of white in the Winter Garden. And there's yet more to this walk than snowdrops. The historic Bridgewater Canal, the attractive Trans Pennine Trail, the pretty estate village of Dunham Town and the herd of fallow deer that roam the grounds of Dunham Massey all ensure that it's an interesting ramble. What's more, most of the walk is on hard surface, and so will be manageable even in the wettest of weather.

CHESHIRE *Year Round Walks*

Terrain Hard-surfaced track, canal towpath, roadside pavement, a short cross-field path.

Map OS Explorer 276 Bolton, Wigan & Warrington.

Starting point Henshall Lane car park (GR SJ 729886).

How to get there & parking Leave the M56 at Junction 7 (A56, Altrincham) and follow brown signs for Dunham Massey. In a mile or so, turn left (signposted to Dunham Massey), and continue past the estate into the village of Dunham Woodhouses. Keep right to pass the Vine Inn, then at the Rope and Anchor, keep ahead to a T-junction. Turn right on Henshall Lane; the free car park is 100 metres further on the right. **Sat Nav:** WA14 5SL.

Refreshments The walk takes you past no fewer than four pubs! There is also a tea room en route, and of course, there are tea rooms and a restaurant at Dunham Massey Hall itself, where you can be sure of classic National Trust fare.

The Walk

❶ From the car park, go through the gate to join the **Trans Pennine Trail**, and turn left. The Trans Pennine Trail is a 205-mile-long cycling or walking route between Southport on Merseyside and Hornsea in East Yorkshire. Maybe this short section will inspire you to tackle the whole some day! After about three quarters of a mile, you reach the first bridge, and there's a decision to make. If you would like to reduce your walk by about a mile and a half, go right up the steps and turn right on the road. This will quickly bring you to Point 3. Just one word of caution: the road has no pavement, and though not busy, there is still some traffic; so take care! For the longer walk, simply carry on along the track for another three quarters of a mile to its end at **Oldfield Brow**.

❷ Turn right along the road, and in about 100 metres, go down the wooden steps to join the towpath of the **Bridgewater Canal**. Turn right, and keep ahead for about a mile to reach the first bridge. In the 1750s, the Duke of Bridgewater came up with the novel idea of creating a water channel to transport coal from his mines at Worsley into Manchester. So successful was this innovation that within thirty years the whole country was in the grip of 'canal mania'. Here, you walk on the western extension of that first canal, opened in 1776.

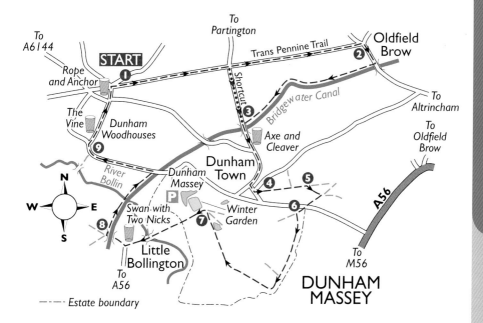

winter

3 Leave the towpath here, and cross the humpback bridge with care. Walk along the roadside pavement, passing the **Axe and Cleaver** pub, and continue into the village of **Dunham Town**. After a right-hand bend (with **Lavender Tea Rooms** on the right), the road forks. Go left here into **Charcoal Lane**, and continue for 100 metres or so, to where **Oldfield Lane** joins from the left.

4 Here, take the signed cross-field path between two lanes. In the next field, keep ahead beside the hedge, then cross a stile into the golf course. Now, go diagonally right to join a tarmacked path.

5 The path bends round, passes a small toilet block, and then forks. Go right, and in about forty metres, a yellow-topped post stands on your right. Look behind you and to the right (i.e., turn through about 120°) to see a similar post on the edge of the woodland. Cross the turf to reach this, then continue through the woods to the road.

6 A ladder stile into the grounds of **Dunham Massey Park** is now diagonally opposite. Cross this stile, and in about 100 metres, go left on a lesser path that leads through the parkland to reach gated enclosures. Keep straight ahead through these, ignoring the path off to the right between them. After a long woodland stretch, where deer often graze, and a lake (**Island Pool**), you arrive

Deer with winter antlers in the park.

in front of Dunham Massey Hall. The **Winter Garden**, with its snowdrops, is on your right here.

7 Leaving the buildings on your right, bear left downhill, and cross another ladder stile to leave the grounds. A hard-surfaced path now leads to a former mill on the **River Bollin**. Cross the footbridge, and continue past the **Swan with Two Nicks** pub. At the road junction, keep right on a cobbled track.

8 Under the bridge, go up the steps on the right, and turn left on the towpath. You now have a canal-side walk of about three quarters of a mile, at one point crossing an aqueduct over the **River Bollin**. A constriction in the canal signals another bridge. Just before this, go down the slope to join the road. Continue left along the pavement to reach the village of **Dunham Woodhouses**.

9 In the village, keep right to pass the **Vine Inn**, and continue to the junction at the **Rope and Anchor**. Keep right here, and in a couple of minutes the Trans Pennine Trail crosses your road. Turn right here, and continue for 100 metres to the car park.

winter

What to look out for –

The snowdrops

The Dunham Massey Winter Garden was planted in 2007, and there are other species, like blue winter irises and witch hazel, to them set off. Entry is free for National Trust members, while others have to pay a fee, but even so, some snowdrops can be seen from outside the garden. Pick your time: the snowdrops appear from mid-January onwards if the winter has not been too severe.

If you have enjoyed this walk

There are many other country houses in Cheshire that offer a display of snowdrops. Perhaps the most impressive is Rode Hall at Scholar Green, but you could also try Arley Hall at Northwich, Cholmondeley Castle at Malpas or Adlington Hall near Macclesfield.

Capesthorne Hall and ornamental bridge.

20 Redesmere

4 miles (6.4 km)

Long, low rays of winter sunlight have a magical effect on water, bringing out a thousand shades of blue on an otherwise grey palette. There's more than enough water on this walk, so just wait for a day when the sun breaks through, and off you go for a real treat!

Redesmere is a lake some half a mile long, well populated by a noisy squabble of ducks, geese and swans along with a few hundred gulls, all of whom are cheerfully supplementing their diets in the vicinity of the parking area. With this lively scene the walk begins, and goes on to skirt the eastern shore of Redesmere. Further on, the ornamental lakes of Capesthorne Hall are reached – Redesmere itself was dug as a feeder for these – and there are splendid views of the red-brick Jacobean-style hall across the water. It would be tempting to linger in these meadows for a picnic in summertime, but for now the walk takes to the country lanes, one of them accompanied along its length by a handsome field path. The final stretch is through woodland above a winding stream, a scene well carpeted with bluebells in springtime. Maybe you should return in a few months' time?

Terrain Woodland and field paths, lanes.

Map OS Explorer 268 Wilmslow, Macclesfield & Congleton.

Starting point Parking area beside the lake on Redesmere Lane (GR SJ 848713).

How to get there & parking Redesmere is situated in the village of Siddington, about five miles north of Congleton on the A34. Heading north, turn right off that main road into Redesmere Lane, and the parking area is about 300 metres along on the left-hand side. **Sat Nav: SK11 9PR.**

Refreshments The nearest pub is the attractive Red Lion in Lower Withington, about two miles to the west of Redesmere. An alternative is the Davenport Arms, a pub and grill with a wide menu in Marton, two miles south on the A34.

The Walk

❶ From the parking area, walk along the lane away from the main road. About 100 metres after the lane leaves the lakeside, a stile in the hedge gives access to a field path. Cross this, keeping left to another stile, and continue on a fenced path alongside a field; the path soon leads into woodland. Emerging behind the sailing club, bear right on a broad, unfenced track. When you reach the top end of the lake, turn left to cross a little bridge, and keep ahead through woodland to reach the A34.

❷ Cross this road with care, and go through a kissing gate on the far side. Now keep to the right-hand edge of the field – soon, there is water visible through the trees beside you – to reach another stile. Once over this stile, you are clearly beside an ornamental lake, with **Capesthorne Hall** across the water and an elegant bridge ahead. After crossing the end of this bridge, you will find the next field has the best view of the house, which is directly opposite. Carry on ahead to leave the field over a stile beside a gate, and come out on **Mill Lane** alongside a bungalow.

❸ Turn right, and keep to this lane as it bends left and subsequently dips to cross **Hackneyplat Bridge** over **Snape Brook**. Soon after the bridge, you reach a T-junction. Some steps on the left here take you up to a fenced field path, hugging the lane and emerging on it from time to time. After half a mile, the

winter

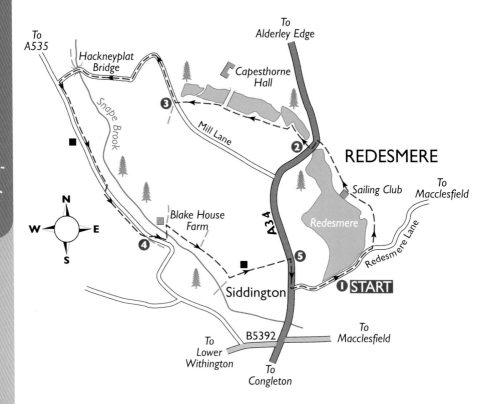

path changes sides, and if you have been tempted to forsake that path for the lane at any point, this is the time to return, because from here it becomes a wide, hard-surfaced track.

4 At a kissing gate, leave the track, and walk on about 100 metres down the lane to take a track on the left, just beyond a house. Arriving at a junction in front of a farm entrance, turn right on a track that passes a cottage and continues as a path skirting woodland, high above Snape Brook. Coming down to a track junction, turn left, uphill, to pass a cottage, and keep ahead on its access road to reach the A34.

5 Turn right on the pavement, and in about 200 metres, go left into **Redesmere Lane** to return to the lakeside parking area.

Beside the parking area at Redesmere.

What to look out for –

Capesthorne Hall

Capesthorne Hall is the private home of the Bromley-Davenport family. It was built in the early 18th century, but time has wrought changes, with various owners adding further embellishments. Today, this Grade II listed building is described as Jacobean in style, and you can admire its balconies, balustrades, towers and pencil-point turrets from across the water. The Hall is open on certain days (see the website www.visitcheshire.com/things-to-do/capesthorne-hall-and-gardens-p28691), and is also a popular venue for weddings and conferences.

If you have enjoyed this walk

There are other lakeside meanders in this book – try Walk 12 or Walk 17. A particularly lovely lake not included here is Budworth Mere in Marbury Country Park, and Astbury Lake, near Congleton, although smaller, it has a path all the way round. None of these can offer you a country house reflected in the waters, though!

OTHER TITLES FROM COUNTRYSIDE BOOKS

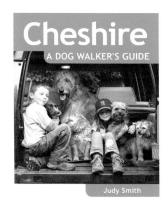

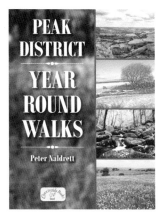

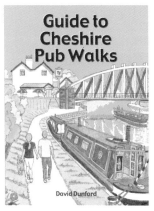

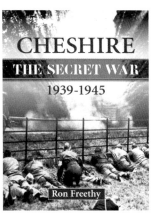

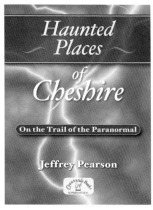

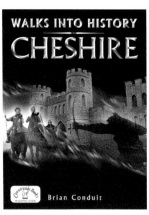

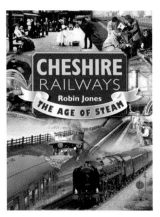

To see the full range of books by Countryside Books visit
www.countrysidebooks.co.uk

Follow us on @ CountrysideBooks